Charles Dickens

Donna Dailey

Foreword by
Kyle Zimmer

CHELSEA HOUSE
PUBLISHERS
A Haights Cross Communications Company ®
Philadelphia

CHELSEA HOUSE PUBLISHERS

VP, New Product Development Sally Cheney
Director of Production Kim Shinners
Creative Manager Takeshi Takahashi
Manufacturing Manager Diann Grasse

Staff for CHARLES DICKENS

Executive Editor Matt Uhler
Editorial Assistant Sarah Sharpless
Production Editor Noelle Nardone
Photo Editor Sarah Bloom
Series Designer Keith Trego
Layout 21st Century Publishing and Communications, Inc.

http://www.chelseahouse.com

A Haights Cross Communications ✦ Company ®

First Printing

1 3 5 7 9 8 6 4 2

Library of Congress Cataloging-in-Publication Data.

Dailey, Donna.
  Charles Dickens / Donna Dailey.
     p. cm.—(Who wrote that?)
Includes bibliographical references.
  ISBN 0-7910-8233-4 (alk. paper)
  1. Dickens, Charles, 1812–1870. 2. Novelists, English—19th century—
Biography. I. Title. II. Series.
PR4581.D25 2004
823'.8—dc22
                                                              2004023885

Table of Contents

FOREWORD BY
KYLE ZIMMER
PRESIDENT, FIRST BOOK

HUMANITY IS POWERED by stories. From our earliest days as thinking beings, we employed every available tool to tell each other stories. We danced, drew pictures on the walls of our caves, spoke, and sang. All of this extraordinary effort was designed to entertain, recount the news of the day, explain natural occurrences—and then gradually to build religious and cultural traditions and establish the common bonds and continuity that eventually formed civilizations. Stories are the most powerful force in the universe; they are the primary element that has distinguished our evolutionary path.

Our love of the story has not diminished with time. Enormous segments of societies are devoted to the art of storytelling. Book sales in the United States alone topped $26 billion last year; movie studios spend fortunes to create and promote stories; and the news industry is more pervasive in its presence than ever before.

There is no mystery to our fascination. Great stories are magic. They can introduce us to new cultures, or remind us of the nobility and failures of our own, inspire us to greatness or scare us to death; but above all, stories provide human insight on a level that is unavailable through any other source. In fact, stories connect each of us to the rest of humanity not just in our own time, but also throughout history.

This special magic of books is the greatest treasure that we can hand down from generation to generation. In fact, that spark in a child that comes from books became the motivation for the creation of my organization, First Book, a national literacy program with a simple mission: to provide new books to the most disadvantaged children. At present, First Book has been at work in hundreds of communities for over a decade. Every year children in need receive millions of books through our organization and millions more are provided through dedicated literacy institutions across the United States and around the world. In addition, groups of people dedicate themselves tirelessly to working with children to share reading and stories in every imaginable setting from schools to the streets. Of course, this Herculean effort serves many important goals. Literacy translates to productivity and employability in life and many other valid and even essential elements. But at the heart of this movement are people who love stories, love to read, and want desperately to ensure that no one misses the wonderful possibilities that reading provides.

When thinking about the importance of books, there is an overwhelming urge to cite the literary devotion of great minds. Some have written of the magnitude of the importance of literature. Amy Lowell, an American poet, captured the concept with her statement when she said, "Books are more than books. They are the life, the very heart and core of ages past, the reason why men lived and worked and died, the essence and quintessence of their lives." Others have spoken of their personal obsession with books, as in Thomas Jefferson's simple statement: "I live for books." But more compelling, perhaps, is the almost instinctive excitement in children for books and stories.

Throughout my years at First Book, I have heard truly extraordinary stories about the power of books in the lives of children. In one case, a homeless child, who had been bounced from one location to another, later resurfaced—and the only possession that he had fought to keep was the book he was given as part of a First Book distribution months earlier. More recently, I met a child who, upon receiving the book he wanted, flashed a big smile and said, "This is my big chance!" These snapshots reveal the true power of books and stories to give hope and change lives.

As these children grow up and continue to develop their love of reading, they will owe a profound debt to those volunteers who reached out to them—a debt that they may repay by reaching out to spark the next generation of readers. But there is a greater debt owed by all of us— a debt to the storytellers, the authors, who have bound us together, inspired our leaders, fueled our civilizations, and helped us put our children to sleep with their heads full of images and ideas.

WHO WROTE THAT? is a series of books dedicated to introducing us to a few of these incredible individuals. While we have almost always honored stories, we have not uniformly honored storytellers. In fact, some of the most important authors have toiled in complete obscurity throughout their lives or have been openly persecuted for the uncomfortable truths that they have laid before us. When confronted with the magnitude of their written work or perhaps the daily grind of our own, we can forget that writers are people. They struggle through the same daily indignities and dental appointments, and they experience the intense joy and bottomless despair that many of us do. Yet somehow they rise above it all to deliver a powerful thread that connects us all. It is a rare honor to have the opportunity that these books provide to share the lives of these extraordinary people. Enjoy.

Author Charles Dickens during his second visit to America in 1867–1868. Dickens was the first celebrity author, who inspired adulation in the same way that today's entertainers do. During both trips he received an overwhelming reception from his readers, who delighted in his novels and admired the rags-to-riches story of his life.

1

Introduction

IN JANUARY 1841, as ships from England docked at New York City's harbor, concerned crowds gathered on the pier and called to disembarking passengers, "Is Little Nell dead?" They were referring to the doomed heroine of *The Old Curiosity Shop*, a novel by Charles Dickens. As was customary of much literature at the time, the story was being serialized in an English magazine, that is, it was published in installments over an extended period of time, and American readers could not wait for the final episode to reach their shores.

A year later, the author himself stepped off the boat for his first American tour. Small in stature, he had long, brown, curling hair and a lively, attractive face. He was nattily dressed in a long-tailed brown frock coat, a red waistcoat with a gold watch chain, and a colorful cravat held in place by two diamond pins. Over this, he wore a fur coat and a beaver hat.

Everywhere Dickens went, there were mobs of people cheering him, shaking his hand, and clamoring for his autograph. They even clipped bits of fur from his coat for souvenirs. Charles Dickens can be considered the first celebrity author, and he was treated much like rock stars and movie stars are today. "I wish you could have seen the crowds cheering the Inimitable in the streets," he wrote to a friend back home.

Dickens was only thirty years old, but already he had become the most popular English writer of his age. At the time of his American tour, he had written five novels and a book of comical sketches. He would write nine more novels and several Christmas stories, including his best-loved work, *A Christmas Carol*. When he died, aged fifty-eight, he was at work on a last novel he knew he might never complete.

All of Dickens's novels first appeared in installments in weekly or monthly magazines. They were illustrated by top artists. Highbrow writers scorned the episodic form as uncultured, but Dickens wanted to be read by as many people as possible. He found that writing in this manner gave him the freedom to be flexible, to improvise, and to quickly turn the story in a new direction if the audience didn't react well to it. He was always aware of his readers' demands and responded to them. In his later novels, which were more complex, he spent much time outlining the plots and rewriting his manuscripts. After they were serialized, his novels were published in volume form.

Dickens began his writing career as a journalist. The instincts to report on and describe people and events in detail never left him. Along with writing novels, he worked as an editor all his life, on a series of newspapers and magazines he had founded himself. In those pages he also wrote articles and essays, and called for reform of the social problems of the day. But his greatest weapon was his fiction, which opened people's eyes to the sufferings of the poor in Victorian England. He attacked injustice, hypocrisy, and other social ills, often incorporating real people and events into his stories and characters.

Comedy and compassion were Dickens's greatest tools. He was highly observant, noting people's expressions and mannerisms in detail, and he had a keen sense of the absurd. He transcribed his impressions into satire through comic characters and situations. But he also wrote vivid, moving descriptions of the wretchedness and squalor of London's poor, and showed great empathy for his characters' human failings and the plight of innocent victims.

Dickens's own life was much like that of many of his characters, a rags-to-riches story. He was deeply scarred by his own childhood poverty, when his father was imprisoned for debt and he was sent to work in a blacking factory at the age of twelve. Even as a famous and successful adult, he carried a deep memory of the grief, humiliation, and hopelessness he had felt. Throughout his life, he drew on his personal experience for some of his most heart-rending scenes.

Dickens's birth in 1812 coincided with the rise of the Industrial Age that transformed England in the nineteenth century. That year saw the launching of the first passenger steamboat, the invention of a machine for spinning flax, and the building of a steam locomotive. During his lifetime, he became the voice of social consciousness, exposing the miserable conditions of the factory workers, miners, and the urban poor, who did not share in the material rewards of that era.

Dickens spent his early years in port towns, and as an adult often escaped to the English or French coasts for long periods. The sea is as central to his work as his urban landscapes. Sailors often feature in his novels, and many scenes take place beside the sea or the River Thames, which runs through London. Fog is another important metaphor used throughout his works, signifying gloom, despair, confusion, and obscurity.

Did you know...

THE VICTORIAN AGE

The Victorian Age was named after Queen Victoria, Britain's longest-reigning monarch. She came to the throne in 1837 at the age of eighteen. Three years later, she married her German cousin, Prince Albert of Saxe-Coburg-Gotha. They had nine children before Albert's death from typhoid fever in 1861. Their family life and strict morality became a model for the nation. Queen Victoria ruled for sixty-four years until her death in 1901. During that time, the population of England and Wales more than doubled, from 15.9 million to 32.5 million people, and there was a major shift to an increasingly industrial and urban society.

In creating his characters, Dickens drew heavily on his own family and acquaintances, expanding on both their positive and negative traits and his own unresolved feelings. But London was his muse. Throughout his life, the city both fascinated and repelled him. His boyhood wanderings filled him with horror and wonder. As a man, he regularly walked ten to twenty miles across the city, working out his story-lines and burning off his restless energy. The city always inspired him, and when he was away from it he often found it difficult to work. He called it his "magic lantern," and it never failed to spark his imagination.

Dickens's novels tell us more about London in the mid-nineteenth century than most history books. He had a phenomenal memory for detail, from the exact color of a lady's dress to the wares in a shop window. His graphic descriptions of prisons, slums, workhouses, dark alley-ways, and fog-covered bridges have given us some of our strongest impressions of Victorian London. We even call such images "Dickensian." Through his caricatures and his use of language, Dickens also captures the great social divide between the classes. A sense of morality, both public and personal, runs through Dickens's works, and in that sense he is a true Victorian. Family life was important in this age. Dickens came from a family of eight, and he had ten children of his own. Although his own domestic life was turbulent, and he examines the unhappiness of family relationships in his books, in the end he upholds the values of the family unit. The virtue of women was also impera-tive in Victorian society; consequently there are no scenes of physical intimacy in his novels, and passion is replaced by intense but innocent longing.

Dickens is at his most moving when he writes about children. Many children suffered in Victorian England, from

The Industrial Age transformed England, driving the population from the countryside to its large cities. Great numbers of the poor took up residence in the Whitechapel neighborhood of London. By the 1840s, Whitechapel had become what is known as classic "Dickensian" London, with its desperate poverty and squalid conditions. This was the world Charles Dickens portrayed throughout his writing.

the child laborers in the factories and mines to the child prostitutes on the streets of the big cities. There were hungry and neglected children living in overcrowded slums, and child abuse was rife in workhouses and boarding schools. Their misery was exposed through Dickens's characters such as Oliver Twist, Amy Dorrit, and Little Nell. In real life, Dickens was a good father to his own children when they were small, though he did become more aloof as they grew to adulthood.

The author's own childhood sufferings forged in him a fierce determination to succeed. He never lost the fear of poverty, and it often drove him to take on more work than was good for his health. At the same time, he had tremendous energy and great enthusiasm for his work. From the beginning, he was very self-assured, and confident in his own abilities.

Dickens was highly disciplined and followed a regular writing routine. He normally wrote in the mornings, followed by long walks or horseback rides in the afternoons. Writers, he believed, should match the hours spent at their desks with equal measures of exercise. Wherever he went, he rearranged his writing desk and room to fit the order he was used to at home. He was very neat and attentive to his personal appearance and expected his household and family to be orderly, too.

Many of the popular writers and artists of the day counted themselves among Dickens's friends. But he had as many contrasts in his personality as the characters in his novels did. His mercurial nature was prone to severe mood swings. One minute he could be laughing and playful, the next he could turn quiet and cold. He was often extremely willful and stubborn, even with his friends. His moods and his great restlessness often made writing difficult.

In public, Dickens was always cool and restrained, reacting modestly to the many honors he received and the tremendous show of admiration from his fans. But among his friends, he was triumphant in his success and enjoyed the applause. Dickens thrived on the interaction with his audience. His ability to move people to tears or laughter gave him a great feeling of power.

Dickens's first love was acting, and even as a child he was a talented mimic and performer. It is not surprising that the dialogue in his novels is highly theatrical. When writing, he often threw himself completely into the characters he was creating, running to the mirror and acting out their movements and facial expressions. He loved performing in amateur theatricals, staging several of them in his own house. Later, he adapted many of his novels for reading from the stage, and gave between six hundred and seven hundred public readings.

In London, a new Dickens novel was often followed by a stage adaptation, usually unauthorized by the author. His most popular works, including *Oliver Twist*, *A Christmas Carol*, and *Great Expectations*, have been made into films, plays, and television dramas.

Unlike many creative people who have difficulty hanging on to their money, Dickens was a good businessman. As his popularity grew and he learned the value of his work, he negotiated better and better terms in his contracts with publishers. He was the first author to insist on receiving a royalty, a payment every time his work was bought, rather than selling his novels for the usual lump sum. In those days, copyright laws were vague, and Dickens suffered great losses from the pirating of his work. While in America, he became the first writer to campaign, unsuccessfully, for international copyright laws. Dickens's readings of his work also made a lot of money, and he set the precedent for modern performers by printing posters and promoting his events.

Dickens was generous with his wealth. Throughout his life he supported many other people, from former servants to family members and friends. His father and brothers, and later some of his sons, frequently fell into debt and relied on him to bail them out. Dickens also contributed to many charitable causes. In Boston, he paid for *The Old Curiosity Shop* to be printed in Braille for the blind. At home, his theater productions and many of his readings were done to raise money for indigent writers and a working men's institute.

Dickens was always very kind and helpful to young writers who he felt had talent, often going over their work line by line. Many of them became contributors to his magazines. He actively sought to raise the status of his profession, and helped to establish the Society of Authors, an organization dedicated to protecting the rights and furthering the interests of authors.

Charles Dickens enjoyed greater popularity in his lifetime than any other English writer had had to date. His novels are brimming with life, humor, and vitality. They still sell in large numbers today, and modern readers find great pleasure and relevance in his books. To understand Dickens's work, it is important to look at the author himself. The genius of his characters and the power of his stories stem from a life as complex and fascinating as those portrayed in his own novels.

In 1817, the Dickens family moved from London to a comfortable hilltop house in the port city of Chatham. Four years later Charles Dickens's father's extravagant spending habits forced the family to move to a cramped dwelling in a rougher part of town. Despite the reduced living circumstances, Dickens considered these as some of the happiest years of his life. The carefree days came to an abrupt end when John Dickens was posted back to London, where he slid ever deeper into debt.

Childhood

IN THE WINTER of 1812, Portsmouth, on the southern coast of England, was a bustling naval port. Britain had become the world's greatest sea power and was keeping Napoleon's forces at bay in Europe. By summer, it would also be at war with America. The rough, boisterous harbor city was home to John and Elizabeth Dickens, who lived in the quieter district of Landport, on the outskirts of the town in Portsea.

Though heavily pregnant, Elizabeth went to a ball and danced into the early hours of February 7. Soon after returning home, she gave birth to her second child, a son. His sister,

Frances Elizabeth, known as Fanny, had been born eighteen months earlier. When the baby was three weeks old, the young family walked along the rural fields to the church of St. Mary's Kingston, where he was christened Charles John Huffam Dickens.

The Dickens's house was small, but respectable. It was simply furnished, with a kitchen and washroom in the basement, a dining room and parlor on the ground floor, and two bedrooms upstairs. The one in which Charles was born looked out over the front garden. There were two attic rooms at the top of the house. Though this modest house has been preserved as the birthplace of the famous author, Charles lived there only a short time.

When he was five months old, his parents moved to a lodging house beside the port. It was the first of many childhood upheavals. Charles's father, John, worked for the Navy Pay Office, and the family moved frequently as he was transferred from port to port. Eighteen months later they moved again, to a larger house in the Portsmouth suburb of Southsea. Elizabeth's widowed sister, Mary Allen, whom they called Aunt Fanny, came to live with them. Another child was born, but the boy died six months later of a condition called hydrocephalus, or water on the brain.

Charles was nearly three when John was transferred to Somerset House in London. It was the child's first experience of the dirty, noisy, urban streets that would later form the backdrop to his novels. The family lived above a grocer's shop in a busy part of central London. John's new job paid less and he began to run up debts.

John Dickens was a jovial, talkative man who wanted to be known as a gentleman. He was the son of a butler, who had died before he was born, and he was raised by his mother, who worked as housekeeper to the aristocratic Crewe family. Lord Crewe helped John obtain his clerical job in the navy. Although John was a kind father and husband, and was conscientious in his work, he was extravagant and irresponsible when it came to money. He loved to entertain his friends and made grand, generous gestures. Throughout his life, he spent beyond his means and was always short of cash. He borrowed money he could not repay and hoped that others would bail him out of his financial troubles.

Elizabeth Barrow, a pretty, educated girl from Bristol, married John Dickens when she was eighteen. She was

Did you know...

DEBTORS' PRISONS

Debt was a crime in England for much of the nineteenth century. If someone was accused of owing money, he or she could be arrested and held for several days in what was called a "sponging house." If payment was not raised, the person was imprisoned indefinitely until the creditors were paid. Debtors' prisons were dirty, squalid places, and many of the imprisoned died from the terrible conditions. The debtor's family normally lived in the jailhouse, too, though they were free to come and go. London's three main debtors' prisons—the Fleet, the King's Bench, and the Marshalsea—were all featured in Charles Dickens's novels. Debtors' prisons were abolished in 1869.

lively and cheerful, with a good sense of humor. With her sharp eye for observation, she often amused her children and friends by imitating the traits and actions of other people. She could also move them to tears when relaying a sad story or event. These gifts she passed on to her son Charles, whose talent for mimicry was unsurpassed.

The family lived in London for two years. Another child, named Laetitia Mary, was born in April 1816. The following January, John was posted to the small port of Sheerness. They lived next door to the Sheerness Theatre, and from his sitting room John would sing along to the choruses of patriotic songs emanating from the stage. From an early age, Charles was exposed to the popular entertainment of the day, which included theatrical farces, comic songs, and naval songs.

A few months later, the family moved to the bigger port of Chatham, in the southeast of England, for John's new job in the naval dockyard there. They took a house at the top of a hill in Ordnance Terrace, a pleasant, breezy part of town. The six-room house was newly built, but somewhat small for the growing family, and the children slept in an attic room, next to the room for their two servants. Mary Weller, who took care of the children, often terrified Charles with scary bedtime stories, one about a Captain Murderer who baked his unfortunate wives into pies. On other nights, she calmed him by singing hymns.

Charles had been a small, sickly boy in London, but in Chatham he blossomed, playing in the fields with the neighborhood children. He was a sensitive child, never very good at games, and was easily hurt by small slights and disappointments. But he was also lively and good-natured, highly observant, and alert to everything around him.

Charles had an almost photographic memory for detail. Even as an adult he could recall his toys and images from his picture books, and the distinct features, dress, and mannerisms of his neighbors. He once remarked that it was a mistake to think that children ever forgot anything. Such a strong and accurate visual memory was unusual. It was a gift he would use to great effect as a writer.

Elizabeth taught him the alphabet, and at the age of six Charles attended a school with his sister, run by an old lady who rapped her pupils on the head with her knuckles. In August 1819, his sister Harriet was born, followed by a brother, Frederick, a year later.

Charles was a precocious child who loved to sing songs and recite poems. He performed comic songs, especially sea songs, with all the attendant attitudes and gestures. He always claimed that he had been born an actor. His parents nurtured his early love of the stage by taking him to neighborhood theaters, where he enjoyed pantomimes, farces, and melodramas, and they gave him a toy theater. John Dickens loved to show off Charles's talents to his friends and sometimes took him to the local tavern, where he would perform dramatic recitations and duets with his sister Fanny on a tabletop.

The four years spent in the hilltop house were some of the happiest times of Charles's childhood. But in 1821 John's overspending caught up with him, and they could no longer afford the rent. They moved down into the streets of the town, near the dockyard.

The dock at Chatham was rough and squalid, full of former soldiers and sailors, dock workers and convict laborers, and assorted ruffians. But Charles liked to walk through the town with his father, absorbing all the sights and sounds of the bustling dockyard. Throughout his life he would be both fascinated and horrified by the low life he saw on the streets.

In contrast to Chatham was the adjoining market town of Rochester, a respectable place with a fine cathedral, castle, and guildhall. It is featured as a setting in Dickens's first book, *The Pickwick Papers*, and his last unfinished novel, *The Mystery of Edwin Drood*.

Charles also took long country walks with his father. One route took them past a fine house called Gad's Hill Place, which to Charles looked like a wonderful mansion. Seeing the boy's admiration for it, John Dickens told his son that if he worked hard and persevered, he might come to live in it some day. It turned out to be a prophecy that came true when Charles bought the house thirty-six years later.

Charles had become a bright, ambitious boy who loved reading. His imagination was full of the adventures of *Robinson Crusoe*, *Roderick Random*, and other popular novels of the time. He dreamed of becoming a successful man. In 1821, he moved to a larger and better school, run by William Giles, where he did well in his studies. The ten-year-old had long, light, curly hair, made many friends, and enjoyed ice skating, rowing on the river, games, and holiday parties.

But the happy times were not to last. In December Aunt Fanny married and moved to Ireland. In March 1822, another child, Alfred, was born. Later that year, baby Harriet died of smallpox. John Dickens's growing debts and the threat of legal action put additional strain on the family. In late 1822, when Charles was nearly eleven, John was transferred back to London to work for the Admiralty. The boy stayed behind to finish his school term, and joined his family three months later. His arrival in London was a shock.

The family took a terrace house in Camden Town, now a trendy part of the capital, but then a new suburb bordered by fields. Charles found it dreary and missed his friends. The house on Bayham Street was small, with only four rooms, a basement, and a garret, where Charles slept. Besides the family of seven, a maid and a lodger, James Lamert (who was Aunt Fanny's stepson), also lived here.

Charles spent his time running errands and cleaning his father's boots. No one considered continuing his education. This was all the harder to bear when his sister Fanny won a scholarship to the Royal Academy of Music and went to live there as a boarder. He lost his main companion. He often walked down Bayham Street, where he could see the dome of St. Paul's Cathedral rising above the smoke and fog of the city. He recaptured that view of the cathedral, to him a great symbol of London, in several of his novels.

Sometimes Charles was taken into London to visit relatives, such as his godfather Christopher Huffam, a rigger who lived near the docks at Limehouse. He was fascinated by what he saw as he crossed the city: the crowded, noisy lanes teeming with street traders, coffee stalls, pie men, gin palaces, shop windows with silks and gold, beggars, gentlemen in top hats, horses and carriages, and the shadowy gas lights at night. He began to wander into the city alone and loved the spectacle of the market at Covent Garden, with the raucous cries of the food sellers and the sights and smells of baskets piled high with produce.

At home, the family was sliding further into poverty. Charles was sent to sell his beloved books, one by one, to try to pay off the debts. He vowed to replace them all and he later did. Mrs. Dickens paid rent on a new house in Gower Street and opened a school, but she attracted no students.

James Lamert had moved on and was now the manager of a blacking factory, which made boot polish, alongside the River Thames. He suggested that Charles come to work for him at a salary of six shillings a week. Just after his twelfth birthday, Charles was sent to the run-down, rat-infested warehouse at Hungerford Stairs, below the Strand, a major road in London. Lamert had promised to give the boy school lessons at lunchtime, and at first he worked in an upstairs room overlooking the river. But soon the lessons ceased, and Charles was sent down to the workroom with the other boys.

After a three-mile walk from Camden Town, Charles worked ten to twelve hours a day, with a meal break at noon and a tea break in the late afternoon. In those days, it was not unusual for a child of his age to work such hours, and many children started work much younger. The job—sealing the boot blacking in small pots and pasting on the labels—was not difficult, but it was dirty and smelly.

Charles was in despair. He felt he would never be clean again. His happy childhood had abruptly ended. "No words can express the secret agony of my soul as I sunk into this companionship," he later wrote, "... and felt my early hopes of growing up to be a learned and distinguished man crushed in my breast."

The worst was yet to come. Less than two weeks after Charles started at the factory, his father was arrested for debt and sent to Marshalsea prison, on the south side of the river in Southwark. Charles pawned the family furniture, including his own little bed, but the small amount of money he raised did not go far enough. The family went to live with John in the prison cell. This was a common practice, and they were free to come and go during the day.

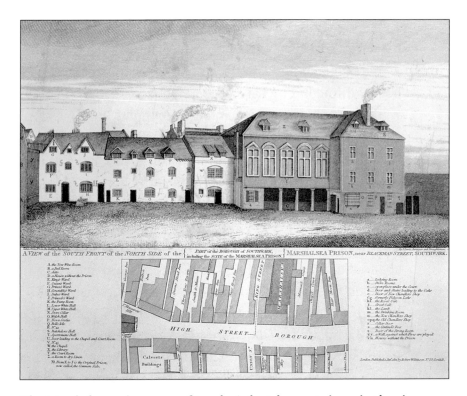

The Marshalsea prison, one of London's best-known prisons in the nineteenth century, was where Charles Dickens's father was imprisoned for debt in 1824. Just twelve years old at the time, Dickens was put to work in a boot-blacking factory and forced to live on his own. The experiences had a profound effect on Dickens, who would provide a vivid portrait of the prison in an early novel, **Little Dorrit.**

Charles continued to live in Camden Town. He wrapped up his wages in separate parcels labeled for each day of the week, which he would spend on food, sometimes using his dinner money to buy a pastry or a glass of ale. Finally, he became so lonely that lodgings were found for him in an attic room near the prison. Every day he would have breakfast with his family in the prison before going to work, then return in the evening for dinner until the gates were locked at 10 P.M.

One day at the blacking warehouse, Charles was struck by terrible pains in his left side. These kidney spasms would plague him all his life during times of stress. He was helped through it by his co-worker, a lad called Bob Fagin, who insisted on accompanying him home that evening. Charles was so ashamed of his father's imprisonment in the Marshalsea prison that when they reached London Bridge, he pretended he lived in a nearby house.

Scenes from the prison and the blacking factory appear several times in Dickens's novels, particularly *David Copperfield* and *Little Dorrit*. He was afraid, during his abandonment as a child, that he might turn into a little thief or vagabond. He drew on those secret images of himself to create the powerful characters of Fagin and the Artful Dodger in *Oliver Twist*. Although the real Bob Fagin was kind and sympathetic, to Dickens the name was a symbol of the evils of the factory, perfect for his fictional villain.

After fourteen weeks in jail, John Dickens's mother died and left him enough money to pay off some of his debt. He was released and the family moved back to Camden Town. Charles also hoped for release, but his mother insisted he continue working at the factory to bring in money. He never forgave her for what he saw as a terrible betrayal.

Finally, John Dickens could no longer bear to see his son as a poor laboring boy. He took him out of the factory and enrolled him in school at the Wellington House Academy. But Charles had already learned his biggest lesson: life was precarious, at any moment his security could be snatched away.

He had spent between six months and a year at the warehouse, but he had feared it would last forever. Even when he became a famous writer, Dickens never forgot the hardships of his childhood and his feelings of shame, misery, and neglect. Nonetheless, it was this same misfortune, and the fear of poverty and disgrace, that drove him to succeed.

At sixteen, Charles Dickens took up what had become his father's profession of journalism. The job of reporter was well suited to the alert and quick-witted young man, who had phenomenal powers of memory and observation. He soon began to write sketches of London street life, published under the pseudonym "Boz." A collection of Dickens's Boz pieces was published on his twenty-fourth birthday. Sketches by Boz *proved an instant success—so much so that he was approached by another publisher to write a large, humorous work. The resulting book,* The Pickwick Papers, *launched the career of Charles Dickens the novelist.*

Starting Out

AT THE WELLINGTON House Academy, Charles quickly became a model student. For the rest of his life, he kept himself fastidiously neat and clean. He dressed well and held his head high, the picture of a lively, healthy, intelligent lad who people took for a gentleman's son. Naturally, he lied about his past, and no one guessed his dark secret.

Charles was back on track to his desired future and cheerfully applied himself to his studies. He carried on his love of theatricals by staging plays in a friend's kitchen, and he wrote stories on scraps of paper for his friends to read. He stayed at the school for nearly three years.

Following his disgrace in prison, John Dickens was dismissed from his job at the Navy Pay Office, though he received a small pension. He got a new job as a parliamentary reporter with *The British Press*. He still had debts to pay, and another baby, Augustus, was born. Soon he fell behind on the rent again and the family was evicted from the house. School fees for Charles and Fanny were no longer possible.

Elizabeth used her family connections to get Charles a job as an office clerk in the law firm of Ellis and Blackmore. He was fifteen, but ready to make his way in the world. The office was in Gray's Inn, one of London's four Inns of Court, which formed the center of the English legal system.

Charles found the job boring and amused himself by dropping cherry stones from his second-floor window onto the top hats passing in the street below. Among his colleagues he was known as a mimic, and they roared with laughter at his imitations of "low" London types, little knowing that he had lived and worked among such people as a child. Through his wanderings, Charles had come to know London and its citizens intimately, from the doctors in Harley Street to the butchers in Smithfield to the flower sellers in Covent Garden.

His time at the law firm left him with scorn for the legal profession for the rest of his life. But his observations of his fellow clerks and the older lawyers gave him a rich font of material for creating Uriah Heep, Mr. Guppy, and other characters in his novels. In *Bleak House*, he exposes the expense, bureaucracy, and injustice of lawsuits and the damage they do to their innocent victims.

After eighteen months Charles left the job and followed his father into journalism. He had already contributed penny-a-line material, such as reports of accidents or fires, to the newspapers while still at school. Now he learned shorthand in just three months and became a freelance reporter, hired to record the proceedings of cases in court.

Charles was soon bored with this job, too. He decided to become an actor. His performances at musical evenings with his sister Fanny were well received, and he

Did you know...

VICTORIAN PERIODICALS

Newspapers and magazines were extremely popular in Victorian times. They had a greater readership than books. A general rise in literacy, improvements in printing technology, and a growing urban society hungry for knowledge and entertainment created an enormous demand for periodicals on a great range of subjects. Serialized fiction such as Charles Dickens wrote was highly popular. The average worker could not afford to buy a full-length novel, but a monthly installment only cost a shilling. Many episodes ended with a dramatic interruption that would ensure readers bought the next one to find out what happened next. High-quality illustrations by leading artists were an additional draw.

had been writing sketches of the characters he met and observed while walking across London, impersonating them to entertain his friends. Some of these observations would one day appear in his novels. He took acting lessons and mimicked the popular performers of the day. Finally, he got an audition at the Lyceum Theatre, but when the day came, he was ill with a bad cold and had to postpone it.

Before he could schedule the audition, Charles was offered a job as a journalist for a new newspaper, the *Mirror of Parliament*, founded by his uncle. His father was also working for the paper. Charles took a second job as well, with an evening paper called the *True Sun*.

Reporting on the proceedings of Parliament, Charles made, in his own words, "a great splash" among his colleagues for his accuracy. The Parliament he observed contained many distinguished men, such as the future prime minister, William Ewart Gladstone. Although these privileged men had abolished slavery and passed some measures of reform, Charles was unimpressed by their long-winded speeches and the workings of the bureaucracy. He was attuned to the sufferings of the poor. When Daniel O'Connell, the Irish statesman, spoke on the plight of his countrymen, Charles was reduced to tears. Throughout his life, Dickens would hold the same irreverence for politics that he felt for the law.

The young reporter plunged into his work with passion, traveling by night coaches, writing as he bounced along, driving himself to be first with the latest news. The hours were long, but Charles was earning good money. He moved to lodgings off the Strand to be near his work on Fleet Street. When he was given more responsibilities at the *Mirror of Parliament*, he resigned from the *True Sun*.

Charles was equally ardent in his personal life. When he was seventeen, he fell in love with Maria Beadnell, a friend of his sister Fanny, who was one year older. Maria had bright eyes and dark, curly hair, and lived with her parents and two older sisters on Lombard Street, next door to the bank where her father worked. Charles courted her for four years, writing poetry to her and exchanging mementos and letters. She flirted with him and charmed him when she played the harp.

Her parents thought him a lively and entertaining young man, but when they realized he was serious, they looked into his background. They were not impressed with his job and lack of social position. Then they found out about his father's time in debtors' prison. They sent Maria away to Paris to attend a finishing school, hoping it would cool their attachment.

Upon her return, Maria had changed. Charles pursued her desperately, but she was cold and did not encourage his attentions. At his twenty-first birthday party he declared his love for her, and she wounded him by calling him a boy. They finally ended the relationship when Charles discovered that she had betrayed his trust by telling their private confidences to a friend.

Charles never got over the betrayal. Throughout his life, he remained oversensitive to any slights or perceived rejections, no matter how small. First his mother had betrayed him by sending him back to the blacking factory. Then Maria cruelly rejected his love for her. He was determined never to be hurt by women again, and this would affect his future relationships and marriage. He developed what he called a "habit of suppression" that made him reluctant to show his feelings, even to his own children, except when they were infants.

Charles poured his feelings into his writing and his characters, but in real life he was repressed. He was forever defensive and protective of his inner feelings, and would not let them show. But like the earlier trauma of his childhood, Maria's rejection also drove him to succeed. He partly blamed his background for the loss, and he was determined to have his own way in the future, to have the power and respect he felt were his due.

On a late November evening in 1833, Charles timidly entered a dark court off Fleet Street and posted his first story through the letterbox of the *Monthly Magazine*. A few weeks later, "A Dinner at Poplar Walk," a sketch of London life, appeared in its pages. Charles received no payment and no author's credit, but he was overjoyed to see his words in print. Moreover, the editor asked him to write more.

Several more sketches were published, and by August they were signed with the pseudonym "Boz," which was the nickname of Charles's younger brother Augustus. That same month he moved to a daily newspaper, the *Morning Chronicle*. He continued writing sketches for the magazine and wrote some for the newspaper as well. His identity of "Boz" was known there, and people started to take notice of this engaging new writer.

Readers were captivated by Dickens's tales of London life. He captured all the characters he had known, the poor, the respectable, and those balanced on the edge. He described the lock-ups and lodging houses, the parlors and city streets where they lived and worked in detail. Because he had felt their fears and desires, his characters seemed real. His great gift was the ability to turn unpleasant scenes into comic situations. These early stories were the prototypes of his later novels.

Charles's confidence and enthusiasm for his work grew. If he was reserved in manner, he was the opposite in his appearance. He bought a blue cloak with velvet trim and a striking hat, and became a stylish dresser.

But his high spirits were dampened by family problems. His father once again fell into debt and was arrested. Charles paid off the overdue bills, moved the family into cheaper housing, and rented rooms for himself and his brother Frederick at Furnival's Inn in Holborn. The rooms were sparsely furnished, since he had spent all his savings paying his father's debts. The family was grateful and impressed by his efficiency, and they came to count on him to bail them out of future troubles.

Charles was now writing for several publications, including his newspaper's sister paper, the *Evening Chronicle*. He became friends with its editor, George Hogarth, and visited him at his home in Chelsea. Before long he was engaged to Hogarth's eldest daughter. Catherine Hogarth was nineteen years old, four years younger than Charles. She was a quiet, plump, pretty girl with dark hair and blue eyes. Her temperament was placid, gentle, and slow moving—the opposite of Maria Beadnell's.

Charles began to meet other important people. William Harrison Ainsworth, a successful author, befriended him and introduced him to his own publisher, John Macrone. The publisher suggested compiling a book with his Boz sketches, illustrated by George Cruikshank, one of the leading artists of the day.

Sketches by Boz was published on Charles's twenty-fourth birthday. It sold so many copies that it was reprinted only a few months later. It received good reviews for its keen observations of comic characters and their mannerisms, its humor, and its sense of the ridiculous. The book was also praised for its powerful portrayal of the wretchedness and vices that ran rife in the city of London.

Soon Charles was approached by another publisher, Chapman and Hall, who wanted him to write a humorous book about amateur sportsmen to be published in twenty installments. When William Hall visited him at his home to discuss the series, Charles recognized the man who had sold him a copy of the magazine in which his first story had appeared. He saw it as a good omen. The publisher wanted 20,000 words a month, for which he would be paid 14 pounds (or £14). Charles told a friend "the work will be no joke," but he found the money too tempting to resist. It would enable him to pay off the rest of his father's debts and to marry Catherine.

Throughout his life, Dickens was intent on making money. His experience of childhood poverty had scarred him, and no matter how successful he became, he always worried about his income and the threat of bankruptcy. Consequently, he always took on more and more work in order to feel secure.

Charles accepted the proposal but molded it to his own desires. He told Hall he would not write about sportsmen, since he had little knowledge of sport, but would write about a subject of his own choice. Hall was impressed with his boldness and self-assurance, and agreed. From the beginning, Dickens asserted his will and independence when dealing with publishers and contracts, always turning things to his own advantage.

Charles knew his head was full of characters. All he needed now was a narrative in which to bring them to life. He came up with Mr. Pickwick as his central character, named after a coach proprietor from Bath whose name Charles had seen painted on the side of his vehicles. Dickens's first novel, *The Pickwick Papers*, had been born.

Charles Dickens's marriage and first literary work, Sketches by Boz, *date to about the same time. In 1836, Dickens married Catherine Hogarth, the daughter of editor George Hogarth. In January 1837, she gave birth to the first of their ten children. Her temperament was placid, gentle, and slow moving—very different from Dickens's seemingly boundless energy, restlessness, and ambition.*

4

Married Life

ON APRIL 2, 1836, two days after the first installment of *The Pickwick Papers* was published, Charles and Catherine were married at St. Luke's Church in Chelsea. It was a small ceremony, attended only by the Dickens and Hogarth families; Charles's best man, Thomas Beard; and his publisher, John Macrone. They celebrated with a cheerful wedding breakfast at the Hogarths' house. Charles and Catherine had a week's honeymoon in a country cottage near Chatham, his childhood home. Then they returned to his three rooms in Furnival's Inn, which had been redecorated to suit a newly married couple.

Charles immediately immersed himself in work. Along with his reporting job and writing *The Pickwick Papers*, he had several other projects on the boil. He agreed to produce a second series of *Sketches by Boz*, and made forays to different parts of the capital to gather material. He signed a contract to write another novel for Macrone, called *Gabriel Vardon, The Locksmith of London*, which would eventually emerge as *Barnaby Rudge*. He penned a political pamphlet lambasting the city fathers, who wanted to ban public recreation on Sunday, the only day off for the working classes. And he was also writing plays and the libretto for an opera by a friend of Fanny's.

Work was always the focus of Dickens's life. The compulsion to take on more projects never left him. He was driven not only by the money, but also by the pleasure of the work itself. It gave him great satisfaction, and he was restless whenever he was not engaged in his work. In spite of his seemingly boundless energy, his overworking frequently brought on health problems.

Catherine resented his dedication to his work and the long hours he spent writing. She was sometimes sulky and suffered from depressive moods. When they were courting, Charles reproached her through letters if he felt she had been "out of temper." Now he claimed that he was working hard for them both, for her comfort and happiness. But in fact, he never considered the effect of his ambitions upon his wife and family life.

Charles loved Catherine deeply. She was his "dearest Kate." He was kind to her family and took them on outings to the theater. But he never confided his deepest thoughts and emotions to Catherine, never told her of the misery of his childhood. His scars from his first painful relationship never healed. He would never bend to anyone else again, not even his wife. He was determined to be the master in his marriage.

The Pickwick Papers detailed the travels of Mr. Pickwick and an assortment of eccentric characters to Rochester, Bath, and elsewhere. It was a type of literature called the picaresque, which involves the adventures of characters who could be called rogues or rascals. Sales got off to a slow start, selling only around 400 copies of the first installment. Dickens was not discouraged and turned his attention to directing the illustrations, insisting on having them done his way. After the second issue, he chose a new illustrator, a young, rather shy artist named Hablôt Knight Browne, who went by the pseudonym of Phiz. He would be Dickens's main illustrator for many years.

With the introduction of the Cockney hero, Sam Weller, in the fourth episode, *The Pickwick Papers* became an instant success. Sales jumped to 40,000. Mr. Pickwick first encounters Weller cleaning boots in the yard of a coaching inn near the Marshalsea prison. Readers recognized the sharp Cockney patter Dickens had picked up in the streets, but it was the first time such dialogue had appeared in print, as it was associated with the poorer, uneducated classes of London. Sam Weller made readers laugh. The novel appealed across all classes, and highbrow readers were said to like it best. It became the talk of the town, with Pickwick hats, coats, canes, and cigars all the rage.

Dickens reveled in his success. He saw a glimpse of his future fame. "Pickwick triumphant!" he exclaimed. He declared that if he were to live a hundred years and write three novels in each, "I should never be so proud of any of them as I am of Pickwick."

The Pickwick Papers had begun like his other sketches, in a light-hearted, reportorial style driven by sharp observations of settings and character. For scenes of Mr. Pickwick's imprisonment in the Fleet jail, he drew on his father's experience in the Marshalsea prison. But as the novel developed, Dickens found his powers of invention coming to the fore. He began to weave his vision of life into his astute descriptions of people and places.

The success of *The Pickwick Papers* enabled Dickens to give up his job as a reporter. But journalism was still in his blood. In 1836 he became the editor of a new monthly magazine, *Bentley's Miscellany*, which carried a mixture of articles, reviews, and fiction. He was paid more than 40 pounds a month and contributed sixteen pages of his own fiction. The job suited him well. He was happy to make his mark on all aspects of the publication and commissioned other leading writers, who he met at literary dinners.

A few days after the first issue came out in January, Catherine gave birth to their first child, a boy. He was born on Twelfth Night (January 5) and was named Charles after his father. "I shall never be so happy again as in those chambers three storeys [stories] high," Dickens wrote, "never if I roll in wealth and fame." In all Catherine would bear him ten children and suffer several miscarriages.

The increased income from *The Pickwick Papers* and other work enabled the family to move to a house on Doughty Street. It was a private road that had a gate at each end and a uniformed watchman in attendance. Catherine's sister, Mary Hogarth, came to live with them as a companion. She was a sweet, delightful girl of sixteen. Dickens developed an innocent but intense attraction towards her. She often accompanied him on social engagements. Frequently, they entertained guests in the evening. Sometimes Dickens would sing his comic songs or act out his mimicry; other times he wrote in a corner with half an ear to the conversation by the fireside.

Dickens began to write a new serial for the magazine, called *The Public Life of Mr. Tulrumble*. But by the second

Charles Dickens's second novel, Oliver Twist, *is the story of an orphan boy who escapes from a workhouse and runs away to London, where he falls in with a gang of thieves. The story was adapted many times to stage and screen, including the 1968 film* Oliver!, *starring Mark Lester in the title role. In this famous scene, Oliver asks the cruel headmaster for additional porridge ("Please, sir, I want some more."), an act that nearly gets him hanged.*

chapter he changed its name to *Oliver Twist*. It was illustrated by George Cruikshank.

The new novel was very different in tone and theme from the jolly world of Mr. Pickwick. Dickens brought his own childhood memories of misery and suffering into this tale of an orphan boy's experience in London. But it was also an attack on the new Poor Law, which made it more difficult for the poor to obtain relief. Dickens had been incensed listening to the wealthy members of Parliament discussing the Poor Law, when they had no first-hand knowledge of the slums, workhouses, and street life. *Oliver Twist* was the first of many novels to use fictional characters to address public issues. It painted the portrait of a world we now call "Dickensian."

With Dickens's success as a novelist came his elevation on the social scene. He was invited to join one of London's exclusive gentlemen's clubs, the Garrick. Other writers sought his company. But he purposefully assumed the appearance of a quiet, modest man, since he was aware of the jealousy in literary society. He also made many friends, who served as an extended family all his life. He was genial and generous with them, and they provided much-needed companionship and support. John Forster, a journalist and critic from Newcastle-upon-Tyne in the north of England, became his closest lifelong friend. He was younger than Dickens, but had a powerful, sage-like manner. In difficult negotiations he regularly acted as Dickens's agent, and helped and advised many other writers. He also wrote Dickens's biography.

Dickens's daily routine at Doughty Street was intense. Each morning he would work on both *The Pickwick Papers* and *Oliver Twist*, and find time to outline a proposal for his next novel, while battling with publishers over contracts and editorial control.

But his domestic happiness was suddenly shattered. On May 7, 1837, after Charles, Catherine, and Mary had returned from the theater, Mary went to bed around 1 A.M. in seemingly good health. Suddenly Charles heard her cry out and rushed upstairs to find her gasping for breath. He sent for the doctor, but nothing could be done. The next afternoon she died in his arms of suspected heart disease. She was just seventeen years old.

The family was devastated, no one more so than Charles. He took a ring from her finger, placed it on his own, and wore it until his death. He kept her clothes in a box in his cupboard for years and dreamed of her every night for many months after her death. He even wished to be buried beside her in her grave, and engraved her tombstone with the words "Young, Beautiful, and Good."

The deep emotions Charles felt for his sister-in-law are one of the mysteries of his character. He idolized her memory and throughout his life was moved by innocent young women who resembled her. She became the model for all the tragically doomed young women of his novels, such as *David Copperfield*'s Dora, and Little Nell, whom he described as "a creature fresh from the hand of God." For the only time in his life, Dickens did not meet his deadlines. Installments of *The Pickwick Papers* and *Oliver Twist* were suspended for a month while the family retreated to a small farm in Hampstead for a period of mourning.

Did you know...

DICKENS HOUSE MUSEUM

The house at 48 Doughty Street is the only one of Charles Dickens's London homes to survive. Now the Dickens House Museum, it offers a fascinating glimpse of the author's life. The rooms are full of memorabilia, from his quill pen to his favorite writing desk on display in the study where he worked. The drawing room is decorated just as it was when he lived there, while the room where Mary Hogarth died contains playbills from his theater productions. In the entrance hall is the only relic of his childhood in Camden Town—the small window frame from his attic bedroom.

The Pickwick Papers concluded in November 1837 with a celebratory banquet attended by all Dickens's friends and associates. The publishers Chapman and Hall gave him a bonus of several hundred pounds. The book had sold far beyond anyone's expectations. Forster helped Dickens negotiate a share of copyright and profits of future sales.

Dickens's social life was a busy whirl of dinners and gatherings in clubs and literary societies. His circle of friends included successful actors, writers, and artists on the London scene. His favorite way of burning off his excess energy was to take long, fast walks across the city, as much as fifteen to twenty miles in one session. He firmly believed that the hours a writer spent at his desk should be matched by hours of vigorous exercise. He also took long horseback rides with Forster.

Brighton and Broadstairs, two seaside resorts, became favorite escapes for the Dickens family. The sea, like the city, was a source of inspiration and renewal. Friends usually came to visit them on their holidays, as Charles did not like to be alone and needed more company than his wife and children could provide. They also made their first trip to Europe. Charles enjoyed it, and in future years he would often go to France or Italy when he felt troubled and stressed in London.

For his next novel, Dickens once again took up the theme of child suffering and abuse. With his illustrator, Phiz, he traveled in disguise to Yorkshire to investigate the notorious boarding schools there. Unwanted or illegitimate children were often dumped in these establishments to endure beatings, rotting food, and flea-ridden dormitories. Dickens saw the graves of many who had died from neglect.

These schools were the model for Dotheboys Hall in *Nicholas Nickleby*. Again, Dickens tempered his wrath with comedy, in such humorous characters as Fanny Squeers. It was a powerful tool. Dickens's exposé in the novel led to the closure of many of the worst schools. Dickens's latent anger towards his mother also came out as he harshly ridiculed her in the character of Mrs. Nickleby.

Another trip to the north took him to the cotton mills of Lancashire and a tour of industrial England. With the harnessing of steam power, cities such as Manchester and Birmingham were transformed into manufacturing centers. Dickens noted the "miles of cinder paths and blazing furnaces and roaring steam engines," but was most moved by the dirty, miserable conditions of the workers in the factories and mines. He vowed to "strike the heaviest blow in my power for these unfortunate creatures," which came with a later novel, *Hard Times*.

Dickens's second child, a daughter named Mary, was born in March 1838. The first chapter of *Nicholas Nickleby* came out a month later. It was a tremendous success and sold 50,000 copies.

Shortly after, Dickens made his first rail journey, by steam train, from Manchester on the newly built railroad line into London. He wanted to be there in person for the publication of *Oliver Twist* in book form, a three-volume edition, which was typical of the time. Although few people did not know by now that "Boz" was Charles Dickens, it was the first time that the author's real name appeared on the title page.

With his first three novels, Dickens set the stage for much of his later work. His fictional London was always described from his inner child's eye, with all the freshness and power of those early impressions. But the city he knew was changing forever, as vast areas were demolished to make way for the train tracks and railroad stations of the new Industrial Age. The railroads, like Dickens's novels themselves, opened up the country to views that had once been hidden, particularly the dark pockets of poverty and the wretchedness of the poor.

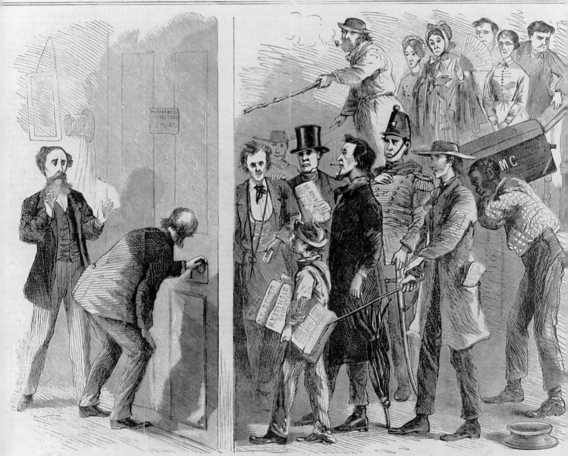

Mr. CHARLES DICKENS AND HIS FORMER AMERICAN ACQUAINTANCES—"NOT AT HOME."—Drawn by C. G. Bush.—[See First Page.]

A distraught Charles Dickens stands with another man behind the door to his hotel room, on the other side of which is a group of Americans angered, perhaps, by their portrayal in Dickens's books American Notes *and* Martin Chuzzlewit. *Dickens is instructing the man to tell the group that he is "not at home." While Dickens admired America and democracy in theory, he felt that American society and politics did not live up to their potential.*

5

Fame and Fortune

IN THE HOUSE on Doughty Street, now home to the Dickens House Museum, there are two portraits of Dickens as a young man. In Samuel Drummond's portrait in the Morning Room, he looks quite the dandy, stylishly dressed and with long, curly, light brown hair. In the dining room, the painting by his friend Daniel Maclise captures him in a more thoughtful pose, sitting at his writing desk and gazing out the window. It was painted in 1839, when Dickens lived in the house, and it was used as the frontispiece for *Nicholas Nickleby*. John Forster's description of Dickens shines out from this painting: "He had a capital forehead, a firm nose with full, wide nostrils, eyes wonderfully beaming with intellect and running over with humour and cheerfulness, and a rather prominent mouth strongly marked with sensibility."

Dickens was only twenty-seven years old and had already achieved monumental success. But he was driving himself too hard, setting himself up for ill health later in life. He suffered recurrences of the kidney spasms he had had since childhood.

In addition to writing his novel and editing *Bentley's Miscellany*, Dickens wrote a couple of farces, which were not very good. Some criticized him for writing too much and too fast. Yet he threw himself into another pet project: editing the memoirs of the great clown Joseph Grimaldi, whom he had seen and admired as a child. Dickens loved pantomime and mimicked clown routines all his life.

John Dickens, meanwhile, was up to his old tricks and had once again accumulated huge debts. He tried to capitalize on his son's success by extorting money from his publishers, selling Charles's old manuscripts and even the signatures from his letters. Dickens was furious when he found out. He paid off the most demanding creditors, then took a coach to Devon, where he rented a country cottage and swiftly packed his parents off to live there.

There were further troubles with his magazine publisher, Richard Bentley. A long-running battle arose over Dickens's contractual rights and payments. As his popularity—and the sales of his books—grew, he continually tried to negotiate better terms and payments for himself as author and editor. Dickens was a shrewd businessman. He knew his worth, and he knew how to market his talent. He was also stubborn, self-assured, and insistent on winning favorable concessions. This inevitably led to disputes with publishers, who were making handsome profits from his work.

With other publishers making attractive offers, Dickens severed ties with Bentley and negotiated new arrangements with Chapman and Hall, whom he called "the best of book-sellers." He proposed a new weekly magazine, which he would write himself and from which receive a major share of profits.

Dickens was now being invited into the drawing rooms and fashionable salons of high society. He met aristocrats and intellectuals, like the great historian Thomas Carlyle, whose philosophical and political writings about social conditions in England influenced Dickens's own political ideas. He was asked to join the prestigious Athenaeum Club, a club for

Did you know...

COPYRIGHT LAWS

Copyright laws protect writers and artists from having their work reproduced without payment or permission. Britain enacted the first international copyright law in 1842, but throughout the nineteenth century American publishers pirated the work of Charles Dickens and other British authors with impunity. Thousands of cheap editions were sold without the permission of the author, who received not a penny. At that time, American publishing was underfunded, with few American authors, and it depended on British fiction to survive. It was only when American authors such as Mark Twain suffered substantial losses and campaigned for redress that an English-American copyright law was enacted in 1891.

scholarly and eminent men. The naturalist Charles Darwin was invited to join at the same time. Dickens never felt inferior in the company of the elite. He saw behind the social masks, while at the same time playing the part required.

Another daughter, Kate Macready Dickens, was born on October 29, 1839. The Doughty Street house was now too small for the growing family and did not reflect Dickens's professional prestige. He took a twelve-year lease on a grand new house at 1 Devonshire Terrace, near Regent's Park, and furnished it with plush carpets, marble mantelpieces, mahogany doors, and fine furniture. He paid particular attention to his library. Always sensitive to criticism, he responded to snipes about his "Cockney ignorance" by creating an extensive library that would impress visitors with his literary taste. He bought books of all the great authors in finely bound editions and rare volumes.

Dickens enjoyed his new social status, though he saw it as somewhat of a game. He dressed colorfully, but was unobtrusive in his demeanor. He hosted parties and dinners at his new home with generous hospitality to his guests, yet he ate and drank modestly himself.

In February 1840, the young Queen Victoria, for whom the Victorian Age is named, married Prince Albert. Dickens watched the wedding procession from the windows of the Athenaeum Club. He carried on a long charade in letters with his friends, pretending to be in love with the Queen. Some declared that he had gone mad from overwork. He may have been expressing the first inklings of marital unhappiness. The many odd contradictions in his character signified the range of strong emotions boiling within, which came out in his powerful prose.

Master Humphrey's Clock was the title of his new magazine for Chapman and Hall. Its first issue sold 70,000 copies and Dickens was ecstatic. But sales soon plunged when the readers realized that they were getting unrelated articles and essays, rather than a new novel.

Dickens decided to enlarge "a little child story" he was planning into a full-length novel and serialize it in the magazine. *The Old Curiosity Shop* was an instant hit and sales of the magazine rose to 100,000. The story of its doomed heroine, Little Nell, captured the hearts of its audience like no other novel had before. Readers were greatly moved by her sufferings and plight, and implored him to write a happy ending. Dickens was deeply affected as he drew the story closer to her death. When Little Nell died, even powerful men wept. The Irish statesman Daniel O'Connell threw the book out the window of a moving train and cried, "He should not have killed her!" But no one suffered more than Dickens. He identified so strongly with his characters that they seemed real to him. He sometimes felt he could see and hear them. When *The Old Curiosity Shop* ended, Dickens immediately began writing *Barnaby Rudge*. Its first chapter appeared in February 1841. Again, the birth of a new novel coincided with the birth of a child, their fourth, a son named Walter.

The theme of this novel presented Dickens with a dilemma. He was now successful and living comfortably, but he identified with the social unrest in Victorian England, where desperate men waited for political reform. Thus he set his story of individuals caught up in the mindless violence of an angry mob a century earlier, during the Gordon Riots of 1780. It was his first historical novel. He alternated dramatized scenes of real events with his usual comic dialogue and pantomime, and pathetic scenes of the eponymous hero in Newgate Prison.

In June, Dickens traveled to Edinburgh, where he was honored by the city fathers and his hotel was besieged by fans. He then embarked on a tour of the Scottish Highlands with Catherine. While traveling he continued to write and file his weekly installments of the novel.

Dickens spent the remainder of the summer by the sea at Broadstairs, a happy vacation with family and friends. He wrote in the mornings and looked forward to finishing *Barnaby Rudge*. At last, Dickens contemplated taking a rest. He decided that if there were a break, his readers would be more eager for his next book. He also wanted to get away.

The pressure of writing weekly, rather than monthly, episodes was making him ill. He developed facial rheumatism and faced an operation to remove a fistula caused by too much sitting at his desk. The surgery was painful, performed without anesthesia, and it took him a month to recover.

Sales of the magazine had fallen during *Barnaby Rudge*. Dickens's publishers agreed to a year's break and to pay him a generous salary in his absence. When he returned, he would write a new work in monthly parts. During this time, Dickens decided to go to America. He had wanted to visit the country for some time. His books were highly popular there, and the American author Washington Irving had promised in letters that his trip would be "a triumph." Dickens looked at America idealistically, believing the young democracy with its high ideals had solved the problems of poverty and privilege that so consumed him in his work. He wanted to witness it firsthand for himself. Catherine did not want to make the trip. She had three small children and a baby, who would have to be left behind. Although she did not want to be separated from them for six months, she was told it was her duty to accompany her husband.

Dickens was excited and spent weeks planning the journey with John Forster and an actor friend, William Charles Macready. He had letters of introduction to distinguished

Americans. He ordered fine clothes for himself and Catherine. They let their house and arranged for friends to look after the children.

On January 4, 1842, barely a month before Charles's thirtieth birthday, they set sail from Liverpool on the *Britannia*, the first steamship to provide a regular service across the Atlantic. Their cabin was so tiny they could not get their trunk in the door. It was a rough crossing, and Charles, Catherine, and her maid Anne were ill and miserable during the two-week voyage.

Finally, they landed at Halifax, Nova Scotia, where Dickens was met by cheering crowds. A similar scene awaited them when they arrived in Boston two days later, and reporters leapt on board before the ship had fully docked. He was showered with gifts and more invitations than he could accept, and had to hire a secretary to handle all the letters and requests. Everywhere he went there were eager crowds who shook his hand, clamored for autographs, and clipped bits of fur from his coat.

Dickens was impressed by the social institutions he saw in Boston: the orphanages, hospitals, and schools for the deaf and blind. But New York was a different story. He was horrified by the slums and prisons, finding conditions there as bad or worse than in London.

In both cities, there were splendid receptions and events where he met prominent citizens. They threw a Boz Ball in New York and composed Boz waltzes. Hundreds attended the Dickens Dinner. But Dickens soon felt hemmed in by all the attention. He could not go anywhere without being mobbed. He had no peace.

At the end of his stay in Boston, at a banquet in his honor, he spoke out on the need for international copyright, a matter of great importance to him and all authors. His work was being published in America without his consent and without any payment. But his speech was not well received. People put him on a pedestal as a social reformer, a champion of the poor, and they wanted him to live up to their image. The following day the newspapers, whose publishers were the ones profiting from his work, called him greedy.

It became a controversial issue for the rest of his stay and changed his view of America. He was frustrated by the lack of public support from those who supported him privately. It made him question American freedom of speech when it came to matters of controversy. Yet he was encouraged by Horace Greeley, a famous New York newspaperman and reformer, who urged him to continue his fight.

Dickens then embarked on a tour of the South and Midwest, but still found privacy hard to come by. In Washington, D.C., he met President John Tyler, who greeted him by saying he was astonished to see so young a man. It was a common reaction. The president's spittoon prompted Dickens to write a hilarious description of the American habit of chewing tobacco and spitting the yellow saliva everywhere—on carpets, in coaches, and out of train windows. He was sickened by African-American slavery in Virginia and white poverty in southern Pennsylvania. He tried to keep fit by walking or jogging beside the coaches and canal boats as they traveled. The wild, remote scenery along the Ohio and Mississippi rivers made a strong impression on him, and he used these landscapes in scenes in a later novel, *Martin Chuzzlewit*.

The party traveled by riverboat to St. Louis. This was as far west as they went. Catherine bore the traveling well, and Dickens was pleased with her. He played *Home Sweet Home* on the accordion for her every night. But he, too, was longing to be home.

Dickens was awed by the spectacle of Niagara Falls, then visited Montreal, Canada, where he felt more at home. He recognized his Englishness was a source of his strength. On June 7, 1842, they set sail for home from New York harbor. This time they enjoyed calm seas and two large staterooms on the three-week voyage.

After happy reunions with his family and friends, Dickens wrote a travel book, *American Notes*, based on his experiences. He finished it in four months. It was both observant and humorous. Though he was critical of slavery, the sensationalism of the press, and other things that had disturbed him, he made no mention of the copyright issue. He praised the people for their generosity and was generally restrained in his criticisms. But the book caused an uproar in America, after the book appeared in pirated editions stolen from the proof sheets.

The book had a better reception in England, where it earned him 1000 pounds (or £1000) towards the expenses of the journey. And his trip had brought him new friends in American writers such as Washington Irving, Edgar Allan Poe, and the poet Henry Wadsworth Longfellow, who visited him in London.

Christmas ends merry for the Cratchit family, including young Tiny Tim, in this movie version of A Christmas Carol, *Charles Dickens's most popular story.* A Christmas Carol *was a runaway bestseller when it was published in 1843 and created a demand from his readers for more holiday stories. In all, Dickens wrote five Christmas stories, none of which achieved the great popularity of the earliest work.*

European Travels

AFTER A YEAR'S break from writing fiction, in 1843 Dickens embarked on a new novel, *Martin Chuzzlewit*. He found it hard to get started and paced the floor of his study for days. Unlike his previous novels, it was based on a single theme, selfishness.

Dickens saw selfishness all around him, from the greed of factory owners to the hardness of those who opposed social improvements. He was incensed by the neglected children he saw in what were called "ragged schools," free schools that provided basic education for the city's poorest youth. Still, the book's early scenes were some of the funniest he had written yet. Its central characters included the great hypocrite, Mr. Pecksniff, and the absurd Mrs. Gamp.

But the public did not readily take to the new novel. Sales were down, and Dickens looked for a way to spark interest. In episode six, he sent young Martin off to America, where he retraced Dickens's misadventures. Angered by the abuse he had received following *American Notes*, Dickens let loose with wicked parody in the American scenes of *Martin Chuzzlewit*. While English readers found it humorous, American readers were furious.

Sales remained low. Dickens fell out with his publishers, Chapman and Hall, over a contractual clause suggesting a reduced payment for low sales. Dickens took great offense, and his fierce pride prevented him from making amends. He sought a new publisher.

On the home front, Georgina Hogarth, Catherine's younger sister, came to live with them. She had looked after the children when they were in America and they were fond of her. At fifteen, she so resembled her dead sister, Mary, that Dickens sometimes felt the good old times had returned. Georgina accompanied him on social engagements when Catherine was confined with pregnancies.

Dickens also involved himself in public projects. He helped found the Society of Authors, which is still an important professional organization today. He also advised the young heiress Angela Burdett Coutts, whom he had met at high society gatherings. She wanted to use her fortune for philanthropic causes. Dickens helped her set up a school for poor children in Holborn and later, a home for "fallen women" in Shepherds Bush.

While he was writing *Martin Chuzzlewit*, Dickens's parents asked him to bring them back from Exeter, and he resettled them at Blackheath in south London. His brothers were also running up debts that they expected him to pay. Dickens needed to bring in more money.

Inspiration came in the form of *A Christmas Carol*. He wrote the story alongside *Martin Chuzzlewit*, and it was intended to warm people's hearts after the harsh realism of that novel. He began in October 1843 and it was finished in time for Christmas publication.

Dickens was excited and consumed by the writing of the tale. Its characters—Scrooge, Bob Cratchit, Tiny Tim, and the Christmas ghosts—were all parts of himself or his personal vision. As he walked miles through the city at night, thinking about the story, he "wept and laughed and wept again." When the novel was finished, there were great Christmas parties and celebrations at Devonshire Terrace, with dancing, dining, magic tricks, and games. The book was a great success and sold 6,000 copies on the first day alone. *A Christmas Carol* remains his most popular story to this day.

Dickens had paid for the publication himself, hiring Chapman and Hall as printers. He had insisted on a high-quality volume, and problems arose over the printing expenses. He made less than a quarter of the 1000 pounds he was hoping for. A pirated edition of *A Christmas Carol* had also done damage to the sales. It was so blatant that Dickens won an injunction for damages, but he never received them because the publishers fled into bankruptcy. The suit had cost him 700 pounds, more profit than he made from the book. It was the only time he went to court over piracy of his works.

On January 15, 1844, a fifth child, Francis, was born. Facing many large, unpaid bills, Dickens suffered an illness, likely brought on by his deep-set fears of poverty. When he recovered, he negotiated an advance with a new publisher, Bradbury and Evans.

Dickens developed a restlessness that was constant and very noticeable. It stemmed partly from his childhood and partly from his increasing dissatisfaction with his wife, which he could not yet face. He decided to spend a year in Italy, where he could be free of regular deadlines and concentrate on one story in its entirety.

On July 2, 1844, Dickens, Catherine, their five children, Georgina, and three servants set out in a large carriage he had bought to transport his household on the journey. Two weeks later they arrived in Italy, where he had rented an old, somewhat shabby, villa on the outskirts of Genoa. He dedicated himself to learning Italian while he waited for his writing desk to arrive from London.

Did you know...

INDUSTRIAL BRITAIN

During the Victorian era Britain became the world's first industrialized nation. Huge technological advances in manufacturing and steam travel changed the way people worked and lived. Thousands moved from the countryside to the new industrial cities to find work. Factory owners and managers prospered, but workers were low paid and easily became destitute if unemployed. Many lived in unsanitary, overcrowded conditions. The neighborhoods of the poor were dirty and noisy, the air filled with factory smoke and soot from hundreds of coal fires. The only means of financial aid was the workhouse, where families were separated into the harsh, degrading regime portrayed by Charles Dickens in *Oliver Twist*.

Dickens was both fascinated and dismayed by the dirty, decaying city, with its ancient statues and monuments, decorative churches, and crumbling mansions, and the sounds and smells of the bustling life in the narrow streets. After three months, the family left the old house and moved to Palazzo Peschiere in the city center. It had frescoes by Michelangelo and a beautiful view over the garden, across the harbor to the Alps.

Dickens tried to begin a new Christmas story, but found it hard to work. He needed the magic he found in London's streets, which evoked the scenes and characters of his novels. At first, the noise from Genoa's cathedral bells irritated him. But then he likened them to the church bells of London, and this proved the inspiration he needed. His new story was called *The Chimes*, and it dealt with a favorite theme: the miseries of the poor on the streets of London, and the need for humanity and justice. Dickens wrote furiously, rising at 7 A.M. and working until 3 P.M. or later. He felt all the sorrow and agitation of the tale as if it were real. He finished it in a month. Then he rushed back to London to read the story to his friends, wanting their opinion. They were moved to tears. After arranging for the book's publication, Dickens traveled back to Paris with his friend, William Charles Macready. He was back with his family in Genoa in time for Christmas. *The Chimes* would be a huge success, relieving his financial worries.

Soon he was off again, with Catherine, on a three-month journey through southern Italy to collect material for a new travel book. They traveled to Pisa and Rome to explore the ancient ruins and monuments, then south to Naples, where he insisted on climbing Mount Vesuvius during a minor eruption to look into the mouth of the crater while it was in flames.

Dickens greatly enjoyed his year in Italy. He liked the warmth and friendliness of the Italians, and they were respectful to him.

This time he was a private traveler, not a celebrity or social observer. Here he was free from those obligations.

The family returned to London, but Dickens had not yet started the next great novel he had anticipated writing. As if to distract himself, he spent the second half of 1845 in other pursuits. His energies were running high. He turned to his old love, the theater, and managed a play by Ben Jonson, *Every Man in His Humour*. He played Bobadil, and his friends acted the other parts. Although their production was amateur, it was a hit and they gave the proceeds to charity. In October, Dickens began to write his third Christmas story, *The Cricket on the Hearth*. On publication it sold double the copies of its predecessors. At the end of October, Catherine gave birth to a sixth child, Alfred d'Orsay Tennyson Dickens, named for his godfathers.

Most surprising of all, Dickens decided to launch a new daily newspaper. He, of course, would be the editor. It was a time of economic turmoil in England. The Corn Laws, which placed duties on imported corn, caused food shortages and put more pressure on the poor. There were riots, and social reformers rallied against the laws. Dickens felt the time was ripe for a radical, pro-reform newspaper to be sold nationally. His friends advised him against it, fearing it would drain his energies and have a negative effect on his fiction writing.

But Dickens was also worried by the poor sales of *Martin Chuzzlewit* and feared his popularity as a novelist might not last. He also worried that his health might fail, so he wanted to grab opportunities when they arose. No matter how great his success, he was always plagued by anxiety over future income.

Dickens had set his mind on it. He found financial backers and hired staff. The first issue of *The Daily News* came out on January 21, 1845. But then, as often happened, he had disagreements with the owners of the newspaper, who wanted more involvement in the daily running of the paper. Dickens wanted to be in full control and could not take any suggestions or criticisms. After 17 days of publication, he resigned and his friend John Forster took over as editor. Dickens continued to contribute essays and articles, including "Pictures from Italy," based on his travels.

Dickens's restlessness was worse than ever. It was a sign that underneath it all he was deeply disturbed. He was unhappy in his marriage, but he felt obligated by fatherhood and social respectability to stay with Catherine. Inside, he felt what he later called "the unhappy loss or want of something." He decided to go abroad again and concentrate on a new novel. It had been almost two years since he had completed *Martin Chuzzlewit*. In April 1846, he signed an agreement with Bradbury and Evans for a new novel in twenty monthly parts.

The family returned to Europe at the end of May. This time they chose Switzerland and settled in Lausanne, on the shores of Lake Geneva. They found a pretty villa covered with roses on a hillside overlooking the lake. Dickens liked to go hiking in the Alps, where he could burn off his restless energy amidst the wild and stunning scenery. A month later, he started on the new novel, *Dombey and Son*.

With this novel, Dickens's writing matured and showed the more complex, ambitious narrative style of his later work. In *Dombey and Son*, a proud London merchant's obsession with his business causes him to neglect his family and destroy everything he loves. The death of the innocent child, Paul Dombey, like the death of Little Nell, moved the nation to tears.

Dickens read the first chapters to new English friends he met in Lausanne. It was received with great applause. It gave him the germ of the idea that he might one day give professional public performances of his work. The writing of *Dombey* went fairly well, but Dickens found that after the long break from writing, he could not work for long periods at a time. Once again, he was missing London, his faithful muse.

He was also having problems with a new Christmas book, the fourth, which he called *The Battle of Life*. But he finished it by mid-October, and it, too, was a success. It was the story of two sisters who love the same man and are both loved by him. The story had parallels with his own life. Its characters, Marion and Grace, even had the same initials as his sisters-in-law, Mary and Georgina.

The first issues of *Dombey and Son* were selling better than expected. But Dickens still found the writing slow. He decided that the problem was Lausanne; it was too quiet, and he needed the buzz of the city streets to spark his creative flow.

The family went to Paris. Dickens hoped the urban environment would inspire him, and he took long walks through the city, as he had in London. They rented a house in the Faubourg St. Honoré during a winter so desperately cold that the water jugs in the room turned to ice and split. Dickens did not enjoy the city on this trip, until Forster arrived for a two-week holiday around Christmas time. Together they took in the sights and met many celebrities, including the author Victor Hugo, who was just beginning his novel *Les Misérables*.

In the new year, they returned to London, and on April 18, 1847, a seventh child, Sydney, was born. Yet Dickens remained restless and dissatisfied with most everything. He even quarreled with his friends. He was always on the move, traveling to and from London to Broadstairs, Birmingham, and Scotland. Dickens himself admitted that he was desperately trying to blow off steam. Once more, he immersed himself in staging amateur theatricals, a very popular activity in mid-nineteenth-century England. The money raised went to benefit needy writers and good causes. He planned, managed, publicized, and acted in several productions over the next year or so. After

Charles Dickens's restless nature drove him to travel constantly. He and his family often visited the seaside town of Broadstairs, where they had a residence. The town is still very much associated with Dickens and hosts a yearly Dickens Festival to celebrate its connection to the writer. Dickens visited Broadstairs from 1837 onwards and wrote the greater part of David Copperfield during his time here.

he had taken the last bow, he was miserable again. He hated staying at home and claimed, "I yearn to be a vagabond."

In this same period, Dickens continued to write *Dombey and Son*, which he finished in March 1848. A year would pass before he could write another novel. In September, his sister Fanny died from tuberculosis, leaving a husband and several children, including a crippled son. Dickens visited her every day during her illness and paid for her medical treatment. This tragedy added to his unhappy state and fueled his desire to escape into fantasy. But he drew on his personal sorrow for his next Christmas book, whose title could have described Dickens himself. Its hero, Mr. Redlaw, must come to terms with painful memories of his past—an unhappy childhood, unrequited love, and the death of a sister. It was called *The Haunted Man*.

The comedian and actor W.C. Fields played Mr. Micawber in this 1935 version of Charles Dickens's autobiographical novel David Copperfield. *Many feel that Fields was born to play Micawber, the unlucky yet optimistic and ever-in-debt character modeled after Dickens's own father.*

Household Words

THE YEAR 1849 opened with the birth of another child, Henry, on January 15. It was a difficult birth, perhaps foreshadowing the painful conception of Dickens's next novel.

By chance, John Forster met an old gentleman who turned out to have known Dickens as a boy. He remembered going with Dickens's father to visit him at the blacking factory, where he gave him half a crown. Dickens was stunned that his shameful past had been revealed. He was so upset that he went home and began to write an account of his early life, pouring out all his feelings of resentment, misery, and fear. This was the spark for

David Copperfield, Dickens's most autobiographical novel. It is the story of a young boy's rise from rags to riches. When he came up with the character's name, Forster pointed out that it was his own initials in reverse. Dickens saw this as a good omen.

Many of the characters in *David Copperfield* are based on real people from his life. The cruel stepfather Mr. Murdstone is the John Dickens who sent his son to the blacking factory. Another aspect of his father appears in Mr. Micawber, with his extravagant gestures and grandiloquent speech. Dora Spenlow is based on the young Maria Beadnell, except in the novel the hero marries her. Other characters, including Peggotty, Uriah Heep, Steerforth, Betsey Trotwood, and Little Em'ly, also have shades of Dickens's past associations. Yet *David Copperfield* was more than autobiographical. Dickens himself called it a complicated interweaving of truth and fiction.

The old kidney pains returned as Dickens dredged up painful memories of his childhood. While writing this novel, he moved the family to a house on England's Isle of Wight, where he felt depressed and high strung. He blamed it on the island, not on the trauma of remembering his childhood. They moved on to two other resorts, Broadstairs and Brighton, before finally returning to London.

The first installment of *David Copperfield* came out in May 1849. It met with immediate success. Dickens finally finished the novel in October 1850. Years later, a few months before his death, he would say that of all his books, he liked this the best.

Dickens was obsessed with the idea of starting a weekly publication. The journalist in him was still very much alive, and he wanted an outlet into which he could channel vital commentary on the issues and developments of the day. Alongside writing his novels, Dickens would work as an editor for the rest of his life. He brought the same degree of talent and meticulous attention to this role as he did to his fiction, and he has been described as the greatest editor of his time. Naturally, he saw the new magazine as a lucrative venture as well. Remembering his previous quarrels, this time he wanted absolute control. Dickens owned half of the new publication, his publishers Bradbury and Evans held a quarter of the shares, with the rest split between Forster and W.H. Wills, a journalist who had worked with Dickens on the *Daily News* and would now be his sub-editor. He set up an office on Wellington Street. His father and his father-in-law, George Hogarth, also joined the editorial staff.

For the title, Dickens chose *Household Words*, a phrase out of Shakespeare. The magazine was a mixture of fiction and social commentary. It included articles, essays, poems, short stories, and serial novels. It covered a great range of subject matter, from theater and entertainment to popular education and reports on scientific discoveries. Dickens himself wrote touching essays about childhood and the misery of the poor in the capital. There were essays on political issues, calls for reform and campaigns against social problems of all kinds. It was a mirror of mid-nineteenth-century England.

Household Words was launched in March 1850. It was highly popular right from the start, with a circulation of 100,000. Dickens, of course, was the main attraction. He commissioned work from leading writers and took great care over every article. He aimed to maintain a "bright" tone. He was constantly engaged in the magazine, and even while on vacation he had articles sent to him and kept in communication with Wills.

The demands of the magazine alone would have been enough for most people. Dickens, however, needed to pour his restless energy into a new cause. With his fellow author Edward Bulwer-Lytton, he aimed to establish a Guild of Literature and Art. Its purpose was to provide financial support for destitute writers and artists. Dickens threw himself into another round of theatrical productions to raise money for the project.

Bulwer-Lytton wrote a costume comedy called *Not So Bad As We Seem*. Dickens produced it and took a leading role. Such was his reputation that he persuaded the Duke of Devonshire to lend his house in Piccadilly for a theater, and the Queen attended the opening night. The troupe then took the show on tour to a string of provincial cities. The amateur production was a hit and made a profit of several thousand pounds.

Dickens was an excellent actor. Given the highly theatrical dialogue in his novels, it is not surprising that he was in his element on stage. Under the glow of the stage lights, he could escape his everyday life and immerse himself in an imaginary world. He loved to hold an audience in rapt attention, to move them to laughter and tears, and to hear the roar of applause. He relished the playful camaraderie of the troupe after the evening performances. Whenever a production ended, Dickens's own spirits fell with the dropping of the final curtain.

In 1851, shadows fell on his personal life. His baby daughter, Dora Annie, who had been named after a character in *David Copperfield*, became seriously ill with a brain disease. Catherine was on the verge of a nervous breakdown and had to leave London for quieter surroundings. And then Dickens's father died. Having undergone a painful surgery without anesthetic for problems of the urinary tract, he passed away soon after, on the last day of March 1851. In his sorrow, Charles forgave his "poor father" for all his shortcomings and failings.

The following month, after making a speech to the General Theatrical Fund, Dickens was told his baby daughter had died of convulsions. She was only eight months old. He rushed home and sat beside her bed throughout the night, only later breaking down. To try to purge his grief, he took long walks through the city at night, visiting the darker areas around prisons, workhouses, and asylums.

Catherine returned, and Dickens took his family away to Broadstairs, the scene of happier times. An air of sorrow hung over their house in Devonshire Terrace, and he decided they should move. Eventually he found a large property in Tavistock Square that suited his purposes. It was in an upscale district, but like his previous residences, it was not far from where he lived as a child.

Tavistock House was badly run-down, and Dickens drew up extensive plans for its renovation. He fussed over the details and was frustrated by the slow progress and casual attitude of the workmen, but it was finally finished to his satisfaction at the end of November 1851. It was now a handsome house, with eighteen rooms decorated to his tastes, surrounded by iron railings with trees and a garden. Still, the experience of renovating it may have influenced the title of his next novel, *Bleak House*.

Dickens turned forty in February 1852 and was feeling the first strains of middle age. That year, despite her precarious mental and physical state, Catherine gave birth to their tenth and last child, Edward.

After a restless beginning, Dickens became engrossed in the narrative of *Bleak House*. Like his previous novels, it was published in monthly installments, but it was much more complex than anything he had written before, with several different themes and intertwining storylines. Dickens attacks the legal system for lining its pockets at the expense of innocent victims and berates Parliament for favoring vested interests over the needs of the common people. This novel also introduces one of the first fictional detectives, in the character of Inspector Bucket.

Bleak House is a dark, disturbing book that lives up to its title. Everything takes place amid images of swirling fog, and there are wretched metaphors of decay and disease in the poor quarters Dickens calls "Tom-all-Alone's." It is one of the longest and most "London" of his books, capturing all the extremes of society and emotion that exist and interweave together in the capital city. From the start, it attracted 10,000 more readers than *David Copperfield* had done.

In addition to running his weekly magazine, Dickens was helping Angela Burdett Coutts with a new project to build cheap public housing, a library, and school in Bethnal Green. He was also dictating *A Child's History of England* to Georgina, dramatizing and moralizing on the country's more colorful historical events. He initially wrote it for his own children, but excerpts were later published in *Household Words*. Georgina had become an important figure in the family. She was nurse and companion to the children, cared for her sister during her frequent illnesses, and played the role of hostess to visitors when Catherine was indisposed.

In the summer of 1853 the family went to the French city of Boulogne, where Dickens rented a large villa outside of town. Friends visited while he continued to write *Bleak*

House. On this trip he developed a strong affinity for France that lasted the rest of his life. He began to dress in French clothing and even grew a mustache.

When the book was finished in the autumn, Dickens set off on a two-month tour of Italy and Switzerland with two new friends, the writer Wilkie Collins, who contributed to the magazine, and the painter Augustus Egg. Collins was twelve years younger than Dickens and, like him, high-spirited. It seemed that by choosing younger companions, Dickens craved to hang on to his youth.

Did you know...

CHILD LABOR AND EDUCATION

Throughout Victorian times, about one-third of the population was under the age of fifteen. Children provided cheap labor for the workshops, factories, and mines of the Industrial Age. They were paid the lowest wages, but families were desperate for what little money they could bring in. Many worked sixteen hours a day under terrible conditions, and some were put to work at the age of five. By 1847, laws were passed limiting work to ten hours a day. Children who weren't working attended day schools or Sunday schools, and the poorest were taught by volunteers in what were called "ragged schools." A national education system was established in 1870.

When Dickens returned to England, he was asked to give public readings of his Christmas books to benefit a working men's institute in Birmingham. Catherine and Georgina accompanied him on his first public readings. He gave two readings from *A Christmas Carol*. Dickens was elated by the audience's laughter and thunderous applause. In his public readings, he literally felt the power of his words. As invitations to read elsewhere flooded in, he considered doing more readings. But for the present he had more immediate concerns. Sales of *Household Words* were in decline. His friends and his publishers encouraged him to begin a new novel in the magazine. Luckily, the idea for the story, as Dickens described it, "laid hold of me by the throat in a very violent manner."

Hard Times was the blow he had vowed to strike years earlier on behalf of the industrial workers in the mines and factories. He had already observed their miserable conditions in Manchester, Birmingham, and other heavily industrialized cities. At the end of January 1854, he traveled to Preston to report on a weavers' strike, where he studied the relations between workers and employers.

Preston became the model for the fictitious Coketown, where Dickens launches his first assault on capitalist values. Through the aptly named characters Thomas Gradgrind and Josiah Bounderby, he exposes materialism, greed, and hard-heartedness, and their sad effect on human beings. It was a difficult subject, and Dickens found it hard to compress the story in short, weekly episodes, something he had not done since *Barnaby Rudge*. He wrote *Hard Times* in under six months, finishing it by the end of July. It was a short book, about a quarter the size of *Bleak House*. It achieved its goal of boosting the circulation of *Household Words*.

At Christmas, Dickens gave three more readings of *A Christmas Carol*. He was both exhausted and restless. As usual, more work was the cure. He was anxious to begin a new novel.

A portrait of Charles Dickens with his daughters Mary Dickens and Kate Macready Dickens. Along with Dickens's friends, his daughters often acted in amateur theatricals staged at the Dickens household. Dickens was a talented actor who relished the opportunity to stand in the spotlight whenever he could. His sense of theater made him a popular public speaker in the later part of his life.

On Stage

EARLY IN 1855, Dickens was sorting his mail when he recognized the handwriting on one of the letters. It was from Maria Beadnell. Now that he was famous, she wanted to renew their friendship. All his youthful feelings for her came flooding back. He sent her an emotional letter, referring to their old romance.

They arranged to meet. Maria was now married to Henry Winter and had two young daughters. It had been over twenty years since he had seen her, and he did not consider that she might have changed. Although she told him she was "toothless, fat, old and ugly," he thought only of the pretty young girl he'd once loved, who had been the model for David Copperfield's bride, Dora.

When they met, he was shocked by the plump, silly, flirtatious woman that she had become. His vision of her was crushed, and he was now alarmed that she had returned his attentions. She wrote to him several times and asked to see him, but he always used work as an excuse to avoid her.

Dickens now rather cruelly used another character to express his feelings about her, in the ridiculous and talkative figure of Flora Finching. She appeared in his next novel, which he'd first titled "Nobody's Fault." It was published as *Little Dorrit*. Dickens began writing the novel during his summer vacation on the coast at Folkestone. When the first issues of *Little Dorrit* came out in December, they immediately brought him his largest readership yet.

The novel is a satire on the bureaucracy and corruption Dickens saw in contemporary society. Prison is the story's main metaphor, and, drawing on his own childhood experiences, Dickens uses the Marshalsea prison as the setting for William Dorrit's long incarceration and the place of his daughter's birth. Dickens's sense of the absurd is in top form with the invention of the Circumlocution Office, a hilarious symbol for the government bodies that excelled at doing nothing slowly.

Dickens had grown increasingly disenchanted with London, and he was dismayed by the country's social problems. He wanted to spend the winter of 1856 in Paris and found an apartment for the family on the Champs Elysées. His work was well known in France through translations of his books. He spoke French well and was impressed by the city's arts, theater, and *joie de vivre*, a refreshing change from the staid respectability of English Victorian life.

Between his work at *Household Words* and his monthly installments of *Little Dorrit*, Dickens made frequent trips back to England. His relatives, the Hogarths, were living at Tavistock House, and he detested their presence there. He complained that they were dirty and untidy and left him unpaid bills.

On one such trip, Dickens was walking with his assistant, Wills, near Rochester and pointed out Gad's Hill Place, the mansion he had admired with his father as a child. By coincidence, Wills sat next to Eliza Lynn, a magazine contributor, at dinner that night and mentioned the house. It turned out she had lived there as a child and was now the owner, and she wanted to sell it. Wills told Dickens, exclaiming, "It is written that you were to have that house."

Dickens bought it. It was not nearly as grand as Tavistock House, but for him it fulfilled a childhood dream. At first, after having it renovated, he planned to rent it or use it on weekends. But he loved it so much that the family moved there for the summer of 1857. Meanwhile, he pursued his interest in amateur theater. Productions were staged at his home in Tavistock Place, and Dickens, who was normally tidy and organized, loved the chaos of his rooms being turned upside down by dressmakers, tailors, painters, and set designers. He acted in an old-style melodrama, *The Lighthouse*, written by his friend Wilkie Collins. Georgina, his daughters Mary and Katey, and other friends were among the cast.

By the autumn of 1856, Dickens and Collins were at work on another production. Collins had written *The Frozen Deep*, a melodrama about a fateful Arctic expedition

Charles Dickens purchased Gad's Hill Place in 1856, and lived there from 1857 until his death. Attached to the home is a greenhouse, constructed by Dickens. He remembered seeing the house as a youth in Chatham, when his father told him—prophetically—that if he worked hard, he might come to live in it some day.

in which an explorer heads off to the wilderness to heal a broken heart and in the end dies in the arms of the woman who had rejected him. It opened on Twelfth Night, the evening of January 5, 1857, at Tavistock House. Dickens took the leading role. His death scene was so convincing that the audience sobbed, and it greatly affected the other actors. On stage, as in print, he had the power to project his own hidden emotions of loss and loneliness onto his characters.

Once again, depression came over him when the play ended and life returned to its normal, domestic order. But that summer, a friend, Douglas Jerrold, died. Dickens insisted on a benefit performance of *The Frozen Deep*. It was followed by a farce, to lift the spirits of the audience after the play's tearful ending. Queen Victoria attended and was so moved by the performance that she requested to

Did you know...

DICKENS'S WORKS ON FILM AND STAGE

Charles Dickens's work was so popular in his lifetime that dramatic adaptations were often staged even before a novel had been completed. Since the early days of cinema, his stories and characters have provided a rich source of material for filmmakers and actors. Nearly one hundred movies were made from his books in the silent era, the years before the late 1920s, alone. *A Christmas Carol* is his most popular story and has been filmed over two hundred times. Nearly all of his novels have been made into films or stage plays. The best known of these in recent times are *Oliver!* (a musical based on *Oliver Twist*), *Great Expectations*, and *Nicholas Nickleby*.

meet Dickens. Amazingly, he insisted on excusing himself because he felt it was inappropriate to be presented to her in farce dress.

They took the production to Manchester, where they had to use professional actresses who could project their voices across the huge hall. Here, Dickens met an eighteen-year-old actress, Ellen Ternan. She, her sister, and mother had been engaged to perform in the play. In the farce that followed, Ellen played the young ward of an elderly gentleman (Dickens) who falls in love with her. It was a fateful role.

Shortly afterwards, Dickens confessed to John Forster his unhappiness with Catherine and their marriage. "I find that the skeleton in my domestic closet is becoming a pretty big one," he told his friend. Divorce was out of the question in those days. Even separation would be difficult for an author who had so strongly portrayed the virtues of family life in his novels. Dickens felt trapped and was in despair.

Catherine discovered a bracelet he had bought for Ellen, when a jeweler delivered it to their house by accident. He reacted angrily to her suspicions and was adamant that all was innocent. He insisted Catherine go with him to call on the Ternans. She obeyed.

An air of gloom settled on the household. As if anticipating the inevitable, Dickens began to speak against Catherine to his friends, though many of his complaints were exaggerated or untrue. The unhappiness at home was so strong that he could not write. His mind turned to the public readings he had always enjoyed doing for charity. Now, he considered doing them to earn money for himself. On top of everything else, he had the extra expenses of Gad's Hill Place to meet. More importantly, he needed to divert his mind from his problems. The sheer physical exertion of a reading tour would be a welcome change, and the contact with an audience would buoy his spirits. After many debates with friends, the approval of Angela Burdett Coutts convinced him to go ahead with his plans.

Dickens employed a business manager, Arthur Smith. He planned to start in London before traveling throughout the country. The first reading was on April 29, 1858. The demand for tickets was so great that ten more dates were added to the six scheduled London readings. The repertoire began with *A Christmas Carol* and *The Chimes*. Later readings featured comic scenes from *The Pickwick Papers*, Mrs. Gamp in full cry from *Martin Chuzzlewit*, and the death scene of Paul Dombey.

But at home a scandal was brewing. Catherine had confided her problems to her mother, and Mrs. Hogarth told her she must leave her husband. Her sister, Georgina, did not agree. She refused to abandon Dickens and hoped her loyalty to him would defuse the accusations of her family. The care of the household fell on her shoulders. But how would that look to the world? Dickens went to live at his office to try and stop any talk of impropriety. It was important to keep up appearances. He wanted to smooth things over and planned to be generous to Catherine.

As they tried to negotiate arrangements, they decided it would be best to separate altogether. Catherine would get her own house and an income of 600 pounds a year. Charley agreed to go and live with his mother, as his duty, though he would miss the rest of the family. Walter, a military cadet, had left for India. Mary, Katey, and the two youngest children were still at home, and the middle ones were away at boarding school. Georgina didn't speak to her sister again until Catherine was on her deathbed.

It would have settled there. But the Hogarths were angry. Mrs. Hogarth and another daughter spread rumors that Ellen Ternan was Dickens's mistress. They also cast aspersions on Georgina. It damaged the reputations of all of them. Dickens, according to his daughter Katey, was like a madman. "Nothing could surpass the misery and unhappiness of our home," she lamented. In his anger, Dickens demanded a written retraction from the Hogarths. Eventually, they complied. But he made matters worse by insisting on publishing it not only in *Household Words*, but also in other newspapers. Soon everyone was gossiping about what had been a relatively contained issue before.

It was very poor judgment on his part. Dickens was almost paranoid in his overreaction, imagining innuendo everywhere he went and fearing damage to his career and character. He prepared a second statement, meant only to be seen privately, but things got even worse when it leaked out and was published to great shock and distress for all concerned.

Dickens continued with his readings. The scandal had not dampened the enthusiasm of his audiences. He practiced long hours in his study, honing the script and developing voices, expressions, and gestures for the characters. On stage he became each of them in turn.

For each reading Dickens wore a bright flower in his buttonhole. He came on the stage to great applause and calmly waited for it to die down. Behind him was a maroon-colored screen as a backdrop, and he used a small reading table with a carafe of water. The readings lasted two hours. Sometimes as many as 2,000 people packed in to hear him. Traveling through England, Scotland, and Ireland, Dickens gave eighty-seven readings by mid-November. He made a profit of more than 3000 pounds.

Dickens still had not put his domestic problems behind him. He quarreled with Bradbury and Evans, his publishers of fourteen years, because he thought Evans had sided with the Hogarths. He severed all contracts with them. When they resisted giving up *Household Words*, Dickens closed it down and started a new weekly magazine, taking all the best contributors with him.

It was called *All the Year Round*. The first edition came out April 30, 1859. The main feature of each issue was an installment of a serial story, and the author was given a by-line. Otherwise it was much the same. But it was a clever move. By the end of the first month it was selling three times the number of copies of its predecessor.

The novel that carried the new magazine through its first six months was *A Tale of Two Cities*. Dickens found the weekly episodes as difficult as ever, with the demands of boiling the plot down into the short chunks. But his interest in the subject and the pleasure of writing it kept him going.

It was Dickens's second historical novel. The story is set during the French Revolution, and the two cities of the title are Paris and London. There are vivid descriptions of the French capital during those turbulent times, but the story focuses on events and noble sacrifices made, with little of the satire and comic characters of his previous books. It is also the story of hopeless passion for a young woman.

Little is known about Dickens's relationship with Ellen Ternan. He was generous to her entire family, sending her oldest sister to Italy to study music with her mother as a companion. Ellen and her sister Maria were set up in an apartment on Oxford Street, where they looked for theatrical work.

Dickens's brothers were again asking him for money, and he'd been supporting his mother since his father's death. He decided to sell Tavistock House. With all its painful memories, it would be a relief both financially and emotionally. Before moving, he made a great bonfire in the garden and burned all his private letters from famous people, making a break with the past.

Gad's Hill Place became his permanent home. He furnished rooms at his office for a London base and later rented houses for part of the year. Dickens did another series of readings in London early in 1859, followed by more readings in provincial cities at the end of the year, when he had finished *A Tale of Two Cities*. He then wrote essays for the magazine. In these stories he revisited his past, with scenes from his childhood, night walks through London, and portrayals of street characters. Themes of loneliness and confinement flow through these essays, as if to mirror Dickens's own feelings. They were later collected in volume form in *The Uncommercial Traveller*.

One of these stories, he felt, demanded expansion. It formed the basis for his next novel, *Great Expectations*, which Dickens began to outline in September 1860. The story is set in Rochester and the Medway Valley, where he lived as a child and where he now made his home. Again, it contains many elements from Dickens's past. Here he looks more honestly at social aspirations through the desire of his young hero, Pip, to become a gentleman despite his humble background. The ex-convict Magwitch, who escapes from a prison ship, begins as his tormentor and becomes his secret benefactor. Miss Havisham, the old woman jilted in love and literally surrounded by the cobwebs of her bitterness, is one of his most brilliant characters. Pip's unrequited love for Estella continues another of Dickens's recurring themes.

In *Great Expectations* Dickens returned to his more familiar style of narrative. It was instantly hailed as one of his finest novels. He finished it by June 1861. Dickens had intended a different ending for the story, to have Pip and Estella part company. But for once he let himself be persuaded to give it a happy ending. His friend Edward Bulwer-Lytton felt the public would otherwise be disappointed. Dickens saw the argument and gave his readers what they wanted.

The author at what would be his last public reading. Note the characteristic flower in his buttonhole, carafe of water, and small reading table. Charles Dickens began public readings of his books in 1858 and gave between six hundred and seven hundred performances during his lifetime. They were phenomenally popular with audiences. Dickens donated the proceeds of many of the readings to charities that he supported.

Last Years

DICKENS'S NOVELS DURING this period contained the theme of unrequited love. Both Sydney Carton in *A Tale of Two Cities* and Pip in *Great Expectations* are thwarted in their passions for Lucy and Estella, respectively. Yet they remain hopelessly obsessed with them, haunted by their desire for the unobtainable. This may have reflected an aspect of Dickens's current life as well as his past. He had once written to John Forster that he had a sense of a happiness he had missed in life, a friend and companion he had never made. It seems clear that he longed for a female soulmate. It is doubtful that he found one in Ellen Ternan.

Little has been recorded about the true nature of their relationship. Comments by his daughter Katey suggest that Ellen brought him as much anxiety and suffering as joy. It may never have been more than an intimate friendship. She was flattered by his attentions and appreciative of his financial support. She, in turn, flattered him. But Victorian morality, and the secrecy and guilt that surrounded their relationship, was a barrier to Dickens's love for her.

Dickens settled her and her family in several houses, eventually providing her with her own house in Peckham. He sometimes stayed nearby under an assumed name. She may have accompanied him on some of his trips to France and Belgium. Gradually, she was accepted as a guest at Gad's Hill Place.

Following the completion of *Great Expectations*, Dickens spent the summer of 1861 at Gad's Hill Place. He had made many improvements to the house over the years. A French actor friend gave him a Swiss chalet as a gift. He erected it on the grounds and turned the upper room into his study.

There were usually many friends and family around for company. Dickens worked in the mornings, then went for long walks through the countryside after lunch, taking his several dogs, including a mastiff, a St. Bernard, a Newfoundland, and an Irish bloodhound. After the walk, there would be cricket, croquet, and other outdoor games on the lawn. In the evenings there were merry dinners with games of charades and memory tests, at which Dickens excelled, and billiards before bedtime.

Dickens's daughters had been the most deeply affected by their parents' separation. Mary, who was twenty at the time, was devoted to her father and did not see her mother again until after Dickens's death. She turned down a marriage proposal because Dickens did not approve.

Katey, who was the same age as Ellen Ternan, was more outspoken. She did not believe Georgina had been truthful about the separation, and she went often to visit her mother. Partly to escape the unhappiness at Gad's Hill Place, she married Wilkie Collins's brother Charles against her father's wishes. He was a pre-Raphaelite painter twelve years her senior. After the marriage, Mary found her father in Katey's bedroom, sobbing into her bridal gown. He knew that if it had not been for him, she would never have left home. Charley's marriage, to the daughter of his old publisher, Frederick Evans, pleased him even less. But by Christmas of 1862, Charley and his wife Elizabeth had presented Dickens with his first grandchild.

Dickens's children displayed none of their father's promise. Charley was not doing well in business. Frank worked at the magazine, but showed little editorial skill. He followed his brother Walter to India. While he was travelling, Dickens received word that Walter had died suddenly in Calcutta from a blood infection, leaving many debts.

In between his writing commitments, Dickens carried on his public readings. He claimed that he needed the money to support his many dependents. But in truth he needed the distraction from himself and the stimulation that performing for an audience gave him. He made a three-month tour in 1861 and gave a London series the following year. In 1863 he traveled to Paris for readings at the British Embassy. He loved Paris for its appreciation of the arts and the fact that it held writers, including himself, in high esteem.

Dickens's mother died in 1863. The same year, he also lost two friends, Augustus Egg and William Thackeray, who had patched up their quarrel and shook his hand only a few weeks before he died. Dickens himself was showing ill health. He had attacks of facial neuralgia. His left foot was painful and badly swollen. It was an early symptom of the arterial disease that would eventually kill him. He did not give in to physical discomfort easily. In spite of claiming to be lame, he went on daily walks, often for ten miles or more. It was another example of his great willpower and stamina. And he continued to pour himself into his work and leisure activities at an exhausting pace.

In the spring of 1864 Dickens began work on *Our Mutual Friend*. It would be his last completed novel. In it he lashes out at the greed, cruelty, exploitation, and, in particular, arrogance of the materialistic middle class. Again, his characters feel the misery of frustrated love. *Our Mutual Friend* is the only one of Dickens's books to have a contemporary setting, but it is among the darkest of his novels. The great dust heaps from which old Mr. Harmon made his fortune are a symbol for the current state of society. Dickens portrays London as a place of hopelessness and destitution, driven by the pursuit of money. The novel's grimness is relieved by a suspenseful plot and diverse characters, and sales of the novel soon rose to 30,000 copies.

Although Dickens now disliked London, it was still the source of his inspiration. Early in 1865 he rented a house near Hyde Park and continued to work on the novel. On June 9, Dickens was traveling home from France by train with Ellen Ternan. Repairs were being made on the line near Staplehurst, and the track had been taken up, leaving a forty-foot gap. The driver received the wrong signal and continued on course at full speed. The train derailed, plunging over a viaduct into the riverbed.

Dickens and Ellen were trapped in a carriage teetering above the wreck. Ellen cried out in terror, but Dickens calmed her, saying that while they couldn't help themselves, they could be quiet and composed. He climbed out of the carriage and stopped two train guards, who recognized him and gave him keys. He got the passengers out of the carriage, then went to help the injured lying along the riverbed, filling his hat with water and giving them sips from his brandy flask. Many were dead or dying. Suddenly Dickens remembered he had left his manuscript for *Our Mutual Friend* on the train. Bravely, he climbed back into the swaying compartment to retrieve it.

The aftershock of the accident shattered him. His pulse was irregular and he had nervous tremors and nausea for days afterward. He never fully recovered from the shock and suffered anxiety and passing waves of terror whenever he traveled. As Dickens was writing *Our Mutual Friend*, his health steadily declined. He suffered chest and stomach pains, and complained of a change in his health. The symptoms were signs of heart problems. But instead of relaxing, his response was to push himself harder.

After the novel was completed, he put most of his energies into his readings. In the spring of 1866 he hired a firm to handle promotion for his tours. His new manager, George Dolby, also proved to be an agreeable companion on his trips. Dickens insisted that there be some good seats for each performance available at a low cost; he had been a champion of the working man all his life, and he did not want anyone to be prevented from attending.

Dickens embarked on another reading tour around the country. He had to travel by train, despite the distress it caused him. He dealt with his fear by playing the clown, dancing in his first-class carriage, and amusing himself with silly antics in the hotel. Even under stress, he kept his high spirits. He blamed his physical symptoms on the rail crash, rather than admitting to any serious health problems.

Dickens made a tour of Ireland. And then, unbelievably, he decided to return to America. He had long considered making a second visit, but the Civil War had interrupted his plans. Now the war had ended, and he was told he could make at least 10,000 pounds there. His friends advised against it, fearing his health would collapse under the strain of such a long tour. Neither could he be sure of his reception, given the hostility of the press during the last

Did you know...

DICKENS SITES IN LONDON

Many places in London are associated with Charles Dickens's life and novels. The George Inn, a seventeenth-century coaching inn, still stands off Borough High Street. It featured in *Little Dorrit*, as did the nearby St. George-the-Martyr church. The Marshalsea prison, where Dickens's father was imprisoned, was shut down in 1842 and later demolished, but one brick wall still remains. Gray's Inn, where Dickens worked at a legal firm, and Lincoln's Inn both feature in *Bleak House* and other novels. Nearby, the sixteenth-century Old Curiosity Shop may have inspired the novel of the same name. Ye Olde Cheshire Cheese on Fleet Street is among several pubs throughout the city where Dickens drank with friends.

visit and the reaction to the American chapters of *Martin Chuzzlewit*. Dickens could hardly bear the thought of such a long separation from Ellen, but it was too dangerous for her to accompany him; her reputation would be ruined if she were seen. His health worsened before his departure; his foot swelled again and he was practically lame. As usual, he denied any illness. But he gave himself away at a farewell dinner, where he could not hide his emotions. When he rose to speak, tears ran down his face as the applause broke out.

Dickens arrived in Boston on November 19, 1867. He received a fantastic reception there and everywhere else he went. Although he still found the constant attention uncomfortable, this time he was treated respectfully and not mobbed. Dickens played to packed houses in Boston, New York, Philadelphia, Baltimore, and Washington, D.C., igniting the same raptures of delight and applause in his American audience. But the punishing schedule of one-night stands up and down the East Coast took a serious toll, and he was weak and ill for most of the journey, rallying all his strength for his appearances on stage.

At a farewell press banquet in New York, he spoke of the generosity and magnanimity of the people and the amazing changes he had seen around him. He, too, had changed. He promised to add appendixes to future editions of his two books that referred to America, correcting his first extreme impressions. On April 22, as he sailed out of New York harbor, he raised his hat on his cane and shouted to the cheering crowds, "God bless you, every one!" In his five months in America, Dickens gave seventy-six readings. He earned 20,000 pounds, but at the cost of his health. He would never fully recover from the tour. Flags lined the road to Gad's Hill Place for Dickens's homecoming. He eagerly picked up his regular life and went back to editing *All the Year Round*. Wills was forced to retire after a hunting accident. But Dickens took on his son Charley as an assistant and he proved so capable that Dickens left him his majority share in the publication.

Henry won a mathematics scholarship to Cambridge, which made his father immensely happy. The most successful of Dickens's children, he later became a lawyer and was knighted. Sydney, however, fell into debt after a promising start as a naval cadet. Both Alfred and Edward failed to establish themselves at home and went off to Australia. Dickens had hoped to be remembered as a kind father. But he was demanding of his children, as he had been with his wife, and they could neither live up to his standards nor blossom in his shadow.

In October 1868, Dickens began another series of readings in London. It was to be his farewell tour, and he aimed to do one hundred readings. His health grew worse, and his sight dimmed in one eye. He was tired, bad-tempered, and had trouble sleeping. One afternoon at Gad's Hill Place, Charley heard a fierce argument in the garden. He found his father rehearsing the murder scene from *Oliver Twist*. He was acting out all of Nancy's terrified screams and Bill Sikes's angry blows. It was the shocking climax he wanted for his next reading.

Fearing for his health, his family and friends tried to stop him from performing the scene. Even Dickens was afraid he might petrify his audience and scare them away. But he insisted on performing it in January 1869. The violent scene did indeed create a sensation. Ladies fainted. Doctors warned that hysteria would break out. It exhausted Dickens and undoubtedly made his health worse. He was portraying Bill Sikes murdering Nancy, but the scene was killing him.

During the tour he became so lame that a doctor advised him to cancel a performance. For once, he obeyed. A few weeks later, in April, he was overcome by a feeling of extreme weakness on his left side. He was on the verge of a paralytic stroke, and all further performances were canceled.

In May 1869, Dickens drew up his will. He left 1000 pounds to Ellen Ternan and 8000 pounds, along with his private papers and jewelry, to Georgina. He provided a small income for Catherine and divided the rest among his children, with small gifts for his friends and servants.

When Dickens prepared the contract for a new novel, he may have sensed he might never finish it. He included a clause to cover a partial repayment of the advance in the event of his death or disablement. The new novel, *The Mystery of Edwin Drood*, was unlike anything he had done before. It is a detective story, concerning the disappearance of the young architect of the title, but it also contains illusionary images and ambiguous themes. The novel begins in an opium den in London's East End, and it is likely that Dickens was taking laudanum, an opiate drug, as a painkiller.

In the early months of 1870, Dickens rented a house near Hyde Park. The first episodes of the novel were once again outselling their predecessors. He planned a short series of readings, hoping that performing would bring him some relief from the pain. Instead, they sapped the last of his strength. He had to lie down, unable to speak, in the intervals between readings. The doctor warned Charley that he must be there every night, to run and catch his father if he faltered and bring him off stage, or he would die in front of them all. But Dickens finished the series. On the last night, he stood in the gaslights, tears streaming down his face, and made his final speech: "From these garish lights, I now vanish for ever more, with a heartfelt, grateful, respectful, affectionate farewell."

A few days later, he had a private audience with Queen Victoria, who, out of great respect for Dickens, stood for the entire ninety minutes of their conversation. Then, at the beginning of June 1870, Dickens left London for the last time. He was happy to be back in the Kent countryside. On June 8, Dickens did not take his usual afternoon walk but continued to work on his novel in the chalet, then wrote some letters. At supper, Georgina noticed he looked unwell, and he admitted he had been very ill for the past hour. As he stood up, he had a stroke. Georgina rushed to catch his fall and laid him on the floor. Servants lifted him onto a sofa.

Doctors were called, but they felt it best not to move him. He remained on the sofa all night and the next day, breathing loudly and slowly. His children and Ellen Ternan arrived, but he did not regain consciousness. In the early evening he sighed, a tear ran down his face, and he died.

Dickens's death came five years to the day after the railroad accident. He was only fifty-eight years old. While preparations for his funeral were being made, a death mask was taken from his face, and Sir John Everett Millais drew a touching last sketch of the author in repose. The historian Thomas Carlyle, who had been Dickens's friend, wrote that his passing was "an event world-wide, a *unique* (set) of talents suddenly extinct."

Dickens had wanted a quiet burial in Rochester Cathedral or a country churchyard. But the family gave in to public demand for a grave in Poet's Corner in Westminster Abbey, where many of England's greatest writers are buried. However, they insisted on honoring his wishes, stipulated in his will, for a private ceremony with no black bows or other mourning symbols to be worn, and plain English letters on his tombstone.

His epitaph lauds him as England's most popular author and a sympathizer with the poor, the suffering, and the oppressed. After the funeral, Dickens's grave was left open for several days, and thousands came to pay their respects. The Dean of Westminster recorded that "many flowers were strewn upon it by unknown hands, many tears shed from unknown eyes."

1812 Charles John Huffam Dickens is born on February 7 on the outskirts of Portsmouth, England.

1823 The Dickens family moves to London.

1824 John Dickens is imprisoned for debt. Charles is sent to work at Warren's Blacking Factory.

1827 Charles begins working life as a law clerk.

1830 First job as a reporter. Meets Maria Beadnell.

1833 Dickens's first story is published in the *Monthly Magazine*.

1836 *Sketches by Boz* is published on Dickens's 24th birthday. First chapters of *The Pickwick Papers* are published. Dickens marries Catherine Hogarth and becomes editor of *Bentley's Miscellany*.

1837 Dickens's first child is born. Moves to house in Doughty Street. Begins writing *Oliver Twist*. His sister-in-law Mary Hogarth dies.

1838 Second child Mary is born. *Nicholas Nickleby* begins publication. Moves to larger house in Devonshire Terrace.

1839 Daughter Kate is born.

1840 Dickens becomes editor of *Master Humphrey's Clock*. *The Old Curiosity Shop* is published.

1841 *Barnaby Rudge* is published. Son Walter is born.

1842 Dickens makes first tour of America. Writes travel book *American Notes*.

1843 Dickens begins writing *Martin Chuzzlewit*. Catherine's sister Georgina Hogarth comes to live with them. Publishes *A Christmas Carol*.

1844 Son Francis is born. Moves to Genoa, Italy for a year. Writes second Christmas story, *The Chimes*.

1845 Dickens returns to London. Writes third Christmas story, *The Cricket on the Hearth*. Son Alfred is born.

1846 Dickens launches *The Daily News* but soon resigns as editor. Moves to Switzerland and begins writing *Dombey and Son*. Writes fourth Christmas book, *The Battle of Life*. Moves to Paris.

1847 Dickens returns to London. Son Sydney is born.

1848 Dickens's sister Fanny dies of tuberculosis. Writes fifth Christmas book, *The Haunted Man*.

1849 Son Henry is born. Begins writing *David Copperfield*.

1850 Dickens launches new magazine, *Household Words*. Daughter Dora Annie is born.

1851 Dickens's father dies, followed by daughter Dora Annie. Family moves to new house in Tavistock Square.

1852 Last child Edward is born. Begins writing *Bleak House*.

1853 Dickens spends the summer in Boulogne, followed by European travels. Gives first public readings of *A Christmas Carol*.

1854 *Hard Times* is published.

1855 Dickens has reunion with Maria Beadnell. Begins writing *Little Dorrit*.

1856 Spends the winter in Paris. Buys Gad's Hill Place.

1857 Stages first production of *The Frozen Deep*. Meets Ellen Ternan.

1858 Separates from his wife Catherine. Makes first public reading tour.

1859 Dickens launches new magazine, *All the Year Round*. Writes *A Tale of Two Cities*. Gad's Hill Place becomes his permanent home.

1860 Begins writing *Great Expectations*.

1863 Dickens's mother dies. His son Walter dies in India. Dickens shows signs of ill health.

1864 Begins writing *Our Mutual Friend*.

1865 Dickens survives railway accident.

1866 Makes reading tour of Britain and Ireland.

1867 Dickens returns to America for reading tour.

1869 Begins writing his last novel, *The Mystery of Edwin Drood*.

1870 Dickens gives his farewell reading in London. Dies at Gad's Hill Place on June 9.

A CHRISTMAS CAROL

A Christmas Carol was first published in 1843. It was the first of Charles Dickens's Christmas books and is shorter than his novels. In this heartwarming tale, the miserly Ebenezer Scrooge is visited by the ghost of his former business partner, Marley, followed by the spirits of Christmases past, present, and future. The experience moves him to change his ways and show kindness and generosity, especially towards his clerk Bob Cratchit and Cratchit's handicapped son Tiny Tim.

OLIVER TWIST

First published in 1837–1839, *Oliver Twist* is Charles Dickens's best-known work after *A Christmas Carol*, and has been adapted to both stage and film. It follows the progress of the orphan boy, Oliver, who escapes from a cruel workhouse and runs away to London, where he falls in with Fagin's gang of pickpockets and is led towards a life of crime by the roguish Artful Dodger and the evil thief Bill Sikes. Eventually he is rescued and discovers the secret of his parentage.

GREAT EXPECTATIONS

Published in 1860–1861, *Great Expectations* is considered to be one of Charles Dickens's finest novels. Its young hero, Pip, helps an escaped convict, Magwitch, to evade the police and falls in love with Estella, the adopted daughter of the recluse Miss Havisham. Later, Pip is secretly aided on his quest to escape his humble beginnings and become a gentleman by Magwitch, but eventually he loses his fortune and learns that wealth cannot make him happy or change who he is inside.

DAVID COPPERFIELD

David Copperfield, published in 1849–1850, is Charles Dickens's most autobiographical novel and his personal favorite. Its hero goes through many of the same experiences as Dickens and eventually becomes a successful writer. Many of the characters closely resemble people from Dickens's own life.

NICHOLAS NICKLEBY

Published in 1838–1839, *Nicholas Nickleby* tells the story of the Nicklebys, who fall into poverty with the death of Mr. Nickleby. Nicholas goes to teach at Dotheboys Hall, but is angered by the mistreatment of the pupils, particularly the orphan Smike. He strikes out against the injustice and eventually returns to London to help his family.

THE OLD CURIOSITY SHOP

The Old Curiosity Shop, published in 1840–1841, is the sorrowful tale of Little Nell and her grandfather, who set off on homeless wanderings through the countryside after falling in debt to the mean and spiteful dwarf Quilp.

THE PICKWICK PAPERS

Charles Dickens's first novel, originally titled *The Posthumous Papers of the Pickwick Club*, was published in 1836–1837. It is the story of the comic adventures of Mr. Samuel Pickwick and his friends on their travels around England.

1836	*Sketches by Boz*
1836–1837	*The Pickwick Papers*
1837–1839	*Oliver Twist*
1838–1839	*Nicholas Nickleby*
1840–1841	*The Old Curiosity Shop*
1841	*Barnaby Rudge*
1842	*American Notes*
1843–1844	*Martin Chuzzlewit*
1846–1848	*Dombey and Son*
1849–1850	*David Copperfield*
1852–1853	*Bleak House*
1854	*Hard Times*
1855–1857	*Little Dorrit*
1859	*A Tale of Two Cities*
1860–1861	*Great Expectations*
1864–1865	*Our Mutual Friend*
1870	*The Mystery of Edwin Drood*

THE CHRISTMAS BOOKS:

1843	*A Christmas Carol*
1844	*The Chimes*
1845	*The Cricket on the Hearth*
1846	*The Battle of Life*
1848	*The Haunted Man*

EBENEZER SCROOGE

The miserly anti-hero of *A Christmas Carol*, whose attitude to Christmas is "Bah, humbug!" He is jolted into changing his ways by visits from the ghosts of Christmas.

OLIVER TWIST

The young hero of the novel of the same name. An orphan, he is cruelly treated in the workhouse and is nearly driven into a life of crime, but is saved by the kindness of others who help him discover his true heritage.

FAGIN

The sly villain in *Oliver Twist* who runs a school for young thieves in the slums of London. His attempts to turn Oliver to a life of crime fail and he is executed at Newgate prison.

PIP

The hero of *Great Expectations*. Ashamed of his poor, laboring background, he aims to become a gentleman and win the heart of the proud, beautiful Estella. He finds that his great expectations do not bring him happiness and learns to value his old friends and home.

MISS HAVISHAM

The wealthy but embittered old woman in *Great Expectations* is one of Charles Dickens's most haunting characters. After being left at the altar on her wedding day, she becomes a recluse, living in a dark room with her moldy wedding cake and wearing her ancient wedding dress. She takes revenge by teaching her adopted daughter Estella to break men's hearts.

DAVID COPPERFIELD

The hero and narrator of the novel of the same name. David's story is based on Charles Dickens's own life. He suffers early poverty and hardship, but eventually finds love and happiness as a successful writer.

MR. MICAWBER

A character in *David Copperfield*, in whose home David takes lodging. He is continually in debt and is sent to debtors' prison, and stumbles through a variety of jobs before emigrating to Australia. He is largely based on Charles Dickens's father.

NICHOLAS NICKLEBY

The hero of the novel of the same name. He sometimes acts rashly, but he is courageous and determined to provide for his family and helps others in need.

LITTLE NELL

The doomed heroine of *The Old Curiosity Shop*. She selflessly cares for her grandfather and endures many hardships before her tragic death at the end of the novel. She is based on Mary Hogarth, Charles Dickens's sister-in-law, who also died young.

MR. SAMUEL PICKWICK

The eccentric main character of *The Pickwick Papers* and one of Charles Dickens's best-loved creations. A retired businessman, he founds the Pickwick Club and embarks on a series of adventures with his unconventional friends and servant.

SAM WELLER

Mr. Pickwick's servant in *The Pickwick Papers* was the first Cockney character in English literature. He is full of humor and wit, and is extremely loyal to Pickwick.

Ackroyd, Peter. *Dickens: Public Life and Private Passion*. London: BBC, 2002.

Ackroyd, Peter. *Dickens*. London: Sinclair-Stevenson Limited, 1990.

Bibliomania—Charles Dickens: *www.bibliomania.com/0/0/19/ frameset.html*.

Charles Dickens Gad's Hill Place: *http://www.perryweb.com/Dickens/*.

Chesterton, Gilbert Keith. *Charles Dickens*. 1906. Online Literature Library: *http://www.online-literature.com/chesterton/charlesdickens/*.

Connor, Stephen. *Charles Dickens*. Oxford: Basil Blackwell Publishers Ltd, 1985.

Daniell, Christopher. *A Traveller's History, England*. Great Britain: Windrush Press, 1991, 1999.

David Perdue's Charles Dickens Page: *www.fidnet.com/~dap1955/dickens/*.

Davies, Andrew. *Literary London*. London: MacMillan London Ltd, 1988.

Dickens, Charles. *American Notes*. London: Hazell, Watson & Viney Ltd, from 1867–68 edition.

Dickens House Museum, 48 Doughty Street, London WC1: *www.dickensmuseum.com*.

The Dickens Page: *www.lang.nagoya-u.ac.jp/~matsuoka/Dickens.html*.

Duncan, Andrew. *Walking London*. London: New Holland Publishers (UK) Ltd, 1991.

Forster, John. *The Life of Charles Dickens*. London: Hazell, Watson & Viney Ltd, (from nineteenth-century original).

Hardwick, Michael and Mollie. *Dickens's England: The Places in His Life and Works*. Great Britain: J.M. Dent & Sons Ltd., 1970.

Horn, Pamela. *The Victorian Town Child*. Great Britain: Sutton Publishing Limited, 1997.

Hutton, Laurence. *Literary Landmarks of London*. London: T. Fisher Unwin, 1888.

Jones, Richard. *Walking Dickensian London*. London: New Holland Publishers (UK) Ltd, 2004.

The London of Charles Dickens. London Transport Executive, 1970.

Mankowitz, Wolf. *Dickens of London*. London: Weidenfeld and Nicolson, 1976.

Online Literature Library—Charles Dickens: *www.online-literature.com/dickens/*.

Porter, Roy. *London: A Social History*. London: Penguin Books, 2000.

Pritchard, R.E. *Dickens's England: Life in Victorian Times*. England: Sutton Publishing Limited, 2002.

Rogers, Pat, ed. *An Outline of English Literature*. Oxford: Oxford University Press, 1987.

Sanders, Andrew. *The Short Oxford History of English Literature*. 2nd edition. Oxford: Oxford University Press, 2000.

Schlicke, Paul. *Oxford Reader's Companion to Dickens*. Oxford: Oxford University Press, 2000.

Smith, Grahame. *Charles Dickens: A Literary Life*. London: Macmillan, 1995.

Tagholm, Roger. *Walking Literary London*. London: New Holland Publishers (UK) Ltd, 2001.

Tames, Richard. *A Traveller's History of London*. Great Britain: The Windrush Press, 1992.

The Victorian Web: *www.victorianweb.org/*.

Ackroyd, Peter. *Dickens*. London: Sinclair-Stevenson Limited, 1990.

Ackroyd, Peter. *Dickens: Public Life and Private Passion*. London: BBC, 2002.

Jones, Richard. *Walking Dickensian London*. London: New Holland Publishers (UK) Ltd, 2004.

Kaplan, Fred. *Dickens: A Biography*. Baltimore, MD: John Hopkins University Press, 1998.

Mankowitz, Wolf. *Dickens of London*. London: Weidenfeld and Nicolson, 1976.

Schlicke, Paul. *Oxford Reader's Companion to Dickens*. Oxford: Oxford University Press, 2000.

Smiley, Jane. *Charles Dickens* (Penguin Lives Series). New York: Viking, 2002.

Stanley, Diane, and Peter Vennema. *Charles Dickens: The Man Who Had Great Expectations*. New York: HarperCollins Publishers, 1993.

www.bibliomania.com/0/0/19/frameset.html
[Online works of Charles Dickens]

www.bleakhouse.ndo.co.uk
[Bleak House Museum]

www.dickensfordummies.homestead.com/BookLinks.html
[Charles Dickens links and resources]

www.dickensmuseum.com
[Dickens House Museum]

www.fidnet.com/~dap1955/dickens/
[David Perdue's Charles Dickens Page]

www.gutenberg.net
[Project Gutenberg, books online]

www.lang.nagoya-u.ac.jp/~matsuoka/Dickens.html
[The Dickens Page]

www.online-literature.com/dickens/
[Online Literature Library–Charles Dickens]

www.perryweb.com/Dickens
[Charles Dickens Gad's Hill Place]

www.underthesun.cc/Classics/Dickens/
[About Charles Dickens]

www.victorianweb.org/
[The Victorian Web]

DONNA DAILEY is a journalist and author. She earned a B.A. from the University of Northern Colorado and later moved to London, England, where she first worked at a magazine located next door to the Charles Dickens House. She has written more than twenty travel guides and books about London, Paris, Ireland, and other cities and countries worldwide, including *Literary London*.